MONTANA 1889

*Indians, Cowboys, and Miners
in the Year of Statehood*

KEN EGAN JR.

RIVERBEND
PUBLISHING

Published by Riverbend Publishing, Helena, Montana

ISBN 13: 978-1-60639-102-0

Printed in the United States of America.

2 3 4 5 6 7 8 9 VP 22 21 20 19 18 17

Cover and text design by Sarah Cauble, www.sarahcauble.com

Riverbend Publishing
P.O. Box 5833
Helena, MT 59604
1-866-787-2363
www.riverbendpublishing.com

Front cover photos
Top row, left to right: Marcus Daly, Louis Riel, Mad Wolf,
Dr. Huie Pock, Helen P. Clarke
Bottom row, left to right: Ella Knowles, William A. Clark, Deaf Bull,
W Bar cattle, Clara L. McAdow, James J. Hill, Dull Knife,
Granville Stuart

To my sons, Devin and Brian—
may history be a guide but never a limitation. . . .

ALSO BY KEN EGAN JR.

Montana 1864:
Indians, Emigrants and Gold in the Territorial Year

Hope and Dread in Montana Literature

The Riven Home: Narrative Rivalry in the American Renaissance

Writers Under the Rims: A Yellowstone County Anthology
(co-editor)

CONTENTS

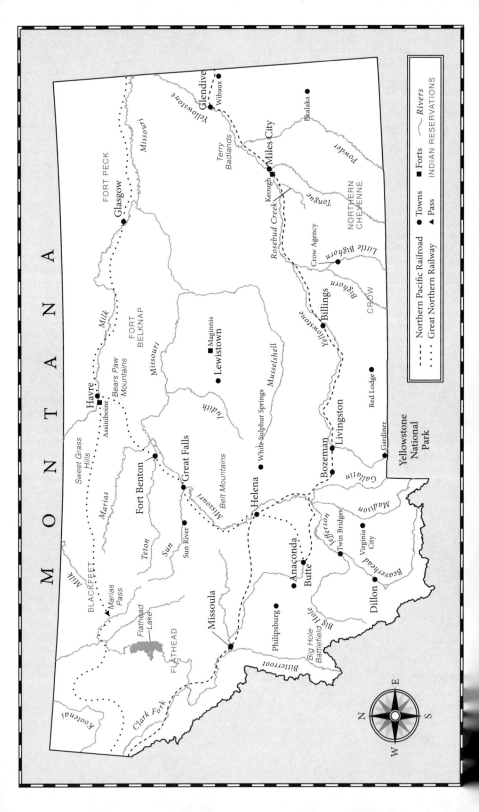

INTRODUCTION

THE AMERICAN WEST WAS BORN ON THE PLAINS OF MONTANA in the 1880s. The West of cowboys and Indians, wide open vistas, freedom from routine and convention, horses sweeping across open plains, that dream vision, that myth, that faith made famous by movies, television, and books was created, in large part, in the territory that would soon become a state.

Montana 1889 tells the story of that invention, for it was and remains an invention, a tale told to reveal and conceal in equal parts. As Montana moved toward statehood, settlers eliminated the buffalo and forced indigenous nations into increasingly constricted spaces; cattle and sheep became the dominant fauna of an area once rich in wildlife beyond our contemporary imagination; railroads bound the region to markets, capital, and culture far away and determinative; and industrial mining on a scale far beyond the fever dreams of the 1860s gold rush came to dominate economy and politics. Yet an entire cultural industry was created to spread that alluring story of freedom and authenticity, the cowboy as symbol of life beyond the bounds of an increasingly corporate, regulated, routine industrial culture. Theodore Roosevelt provides an elegiac rendering of the myth in 1888:

> In its present form stock-raising on the plains is doomed, and can hardly outlast the century. The great free ranches, with their barbarous, picturesque, and curiously fascinating surroundings, mark a primitive stage of existence as surely as do the great tracts of primeval forests, and like the latter must pass away before the onward march of our

people; and we who have felt the charm of the life, and have exulted in its abounding vigor and its bold, restless freedom, will not only regret its passing for our own sakes, but must also feel real sorrow that those who come after us are not to see, as we have seen, what is perhaps the pleasantest, healthiest, and most exciting phase of American existence.

Figures out of Montana such as Charlie Russell, "Teddy Blue" Abbott, and Calamity Jane played their parts in creating this myth, though they often resisted and even ridiculed idealized images of their western lives. In fact, Russell and Abbott were exceptionally astute about the source and folly of the western American myth. As Abbott averred, "I did get to be a cowboy . . . and as Charlie Russell used to say, we were just white Indians anyway." In that memorable statement, Russell names how American culture converted cowboys into stand-ins for the native peoples conveniently confined. To become a white Indian is to hold onto the power of an intense connection to the natural world while concealing the brute reality of displacement and domination.

This book tells the many stories of that transformation, entering into the lives, emotions, and decisions of diverse peoples coming together to make a place now known as "Montana." If *Montana 1864* narrates the rapid arrival of emigrants in an emerging territory at the height of the Civil War and the clash of nations inevitably following from that movement, *Montana 1889* tells how determined men and women set about imposing an American logic, an American grid on the place on a scale unimaginable to those first arrivals at the moment a territory was born. Figures such as William Andrews Clark, Samuel Hauser, Wilbur Fisk Sanders, Granville Stuart, and James Fergus will return, but taking on an altogether different cast, for they will have advanced in time and status and will seek the means to convert early arrival and bitter experience into wealth and power. These early emigrants will be joined by ambitious individuals such as Marcus Daly, A. B. Hammond, and James J. Hill who were astute about the inside games of corporate capitalism and ruthless in advancing their interests in the face of competing desires.

In this way, *Montana 1889* will show the creation of Indian reservations residing within the state borders (they are in fact sovereign nations); the complex, innovative, baffled, surprising responses of native peoples to this new condition of living; the explosion of Butte as silver and copper became the dominant metals; the laying of railroad track that made the transformation possible; the emergence of towns such as Great Falls and Billings, products of those very railroads and of the increasing reach of the Butte mining powers; the creation of Montana's ranching industry, led by charismatic individuals such as Pierre Wibaux; the stories of many women who adapted to this tough place, often in unexpected, powerful ways; the role of many ethnic and racial minorities in a state that can appear monocultural in present times; and the invention of a myth to acknowledge these vast changes and at the same time hide their more disturbing elements. These stories will be told month by month, showing the flow and friction of events and the unfolding destiny of individuals and nations.

I pay special attention to the ways in which Indian nations responded to the catastrophe of the reservation system. In one sense, history simply stopped during the 1880s, for as Plenty Coups, Crow leader, famously said, "After this nothing happened." Yet something extraordinary did happen. Despite the Americans' stubborn attempts to destroy Indian nations through a whole technology of "civilizing," those nations continue today. The reader will discover that resourceful indigenous peoples developed a series of strategies to defeat the dominant culture's best attempts to erase them. Former enemies often traveled from reservation to reservation sharing knowledge, tactics, and encouragement. Most famously, the Ghost Dance or Messiah Craze will be carried to the tribal nations in Montana by 1889, holding the prospect of rebirth and renewal. Despite agents' best attempts to prevent the people from participating, the Gros Ventre, Assiniboine, and Cheyenne will put the dance to use, though in ways far less dramatic than on the Pine Ridge Reservation. Indian peoples also innovated ways to translate defining virtues such as courage and generosity into new rituals, in that way coopting American customs. Natives learned as they went, observing agents' habits and preferences and often manipulating those individuals to achieve both short- and long-term successes. Many leaders took the long view, recognizing the pain and trauma of the present moment, the apparent loss of so much that made them a people, yet knowing history—deep time—can yield a surprising reversal. Most simply and movingly, the people remained a people, dedicated to their nations despite unavoidable conflicts over strategies for dealing with the persistent if clumsy imperialists.

History demands humility of the historian, for it is often tempting to name the winners and losers, the wise and the foolish, the visionaries and the blind. Looking back to that moment of statehood, this writer has frequently wondered about the choices of individuals who were betting on time and opportunity with limited knowledge of all the factors in play. Take Plenty Coups, who would become one of the most famous surviving chiefs from the pre-reservation era. As this book will reveal, he made choices about how to deal with the invaders and their increasingly controlling actions and institutions, choices that might at first blush be labeled "collaborationist" or even defeatist. Yet how arrogant to make that casual charge, typing on a computer and sipping coffee in a house built on Salish land, never having faced the extreme deprivation and soul-killing reality of the early reservation, the life source erased, the defining customs of a life debarred, the power to control one's destiny denied, one's own language ridiculed. Or take the case of Granville Stuart, "Mr. Montana," who, as we will see, chose to turn his back on his mixed-race family to enter into a more "respectable" marriage to a young white woman following the death of his Shoshone spouse, Awbonnie. Easy enough to charge the man with betrayal, yet when have I as a contemporary been compelled to navigate an increasingly restricted understanding of what is proper, appropriate, even "civilized" in conducting one's personal life? Writing history calls forth empathy, then, a willingness to feel outside one's skin to inhabit, briefly and incompletely, the lived experience of human beings negotiating terrain they could barely glimpse, let alone understand and control.

VISIONS

I have not told you half that happened when I was young. . . . I can think back and tell you much more of war and horse stealing. But when the buffalo went away the hearts of my people fell to the ground, and they could not lift them up again. After this nothing happened. There was little singing anywhere. Besides. . . you know that part of my life as well as I do. You saw what happened to us when the buffalo went away.

PLENTY COUPS SPEAKING TO FRANK LINDERMAN, 1930

The reservation system belongs to "a vanishing state of things" and must soon cease to exist. . . . The logic of events demands the absorption of the Indians into our national life, not as Indians, but as American citizens. . . [T]he relations of the Indians to the Government must rest solely upon the full recognition of their individuality. . . . The Indians must conform to "the white man's ways," peaceably if they will, forcibly if they must. . . . They can not escape it, and must either conform to it or be crushed by it.

T. J. MORGAN, COMMISSIONER OF INDIAN AFFAIRS, 1889

Montana has undoubtedly the best grazing grounds in America. . . . The Yellowstone, Big Horn, Tongue River, and Powder River regions contain the maximum of advantages to the cattle grower. Except on the Upper Yellowstone, few herds are yet located in eastern Montana, but in the future the O'Connors, Kings, Kennedys, Hitsons, and Chisholms of the West will be found on the Yellowstone, Big Horn, and Powder River countries of Montana.

JAMES S. BRISBIN, *THE BEEF BONANZA; OR, HOW TO GET RICH ON THE PLAINS*, 1881

[W]e have a country where the white breast has never been disturbed, plenty of ducks, geese, & brant. Elk, moose, and deer in the valleys and bighorn mountain goats & grizzly bear in the mountains, with first class trout fishing in the streams. . . . [P]lenty of the best quality coal, iron, limestone, lead, copper, silver and gold—and all in as fine an agricultural country as there is on the continent.

JAMES J. HILL, PRESIDENT,
GREAT NORTHERN RAILWAY, 1888

The adoption of the [Montana State] Constitution will secure our admission upon equal footing with the original States; it will give us adequate Courts for the administration of justice; it will permit us to tax large quantities of land now exempt from taxation; it will give us the immediate benefit of school and other lands donated by the United States; it will relieve us of that unjust inhibition by which we are prohibited from selling our mines in foreign markets; it will give us a representative in Congress and two United States Senators to represent us in Washington; it will give us the right of suffrage in national elections; it will give us a stable government; it will invite capital and emigration, in short it will break the shackles of territorial bondage and elevate us to the full dignity of American citizenship.

"ADDRESS TO THE PEOPLE" ACCOMPANYING MONTANA
CONSTITUTION UP FOR VOTE, 1889

Linderman later reported that on this occasion [of Montana statehood] Alvin Lee, with whom he worked, said, "Now she's gone to hell"; and he added, "And I believed him."

FRANK LINDERMAN, *RECOLLECTIONS*, CA. 1930

JANUARY

In which Young Man Afraid of His Horses seeks to visit his Crow relatives, Marcus Daly swears off politics, and Governor Leslie harangues the final territorial legislature.

With its mines of wealth, before which the fabled stores of Aladdin's cave sink into insignificance, and its thousands of yet undeveloped treasure stores, who can predict the glory of the future Montana, and who can define its possibilities? It is here that the oppressed poor of the overcrowded sections can find peace and plenty, and it is here where those already blessed with wealth and prosperity can increase their stores. To the laborer, the mechanic, the miner, the capitalist, to the speculator and to the proletarian, seeking a modest home and modest income, Montana offers advantages unsurpassed in the world, and which, if embraced, will satisfy all their wants and ease all their cravings.

YOUNG MAN AFRAID OF HIS HORSES DICTATES A LETTER to General George Crook, demanding permission to journey from his Lakota reservation in Dakota Territory to the Crow Reservation in Montana: "I want to visit the Crows and plan with them for the protection of our people . . . for the white man is crowding us, and will want to crowd us still more." Having become "as one nation, related to each other," the former enemies will "talk of things that are of interest, and what is best for our common welfare." He pleads his case by pointing out "I have relatives among the Crows by the marriage of my aunt.

Young Man Afraid of His Horses at Pine Ridge Agency, 1891. National Archives and Records Administration

. . . They gave me three horses and I want to get them." Young Man Afraid of His Horses is not just any enemy—he played a prominent part in the Battle of Arrow Creek in August of 1864, a determined effort by the Lakota, Cheyenne, and Arapaho to decimate an Apsáalooke encampment near present-day Pryor. That famous battle was a result of early incursions by white emigrants, forcing the Lakota and their allies farther west in pursuit of prime hunting grounds. Now that same proud warrior desires to commune with the Crows. Nannie Alderson, wife of an early rancher in southeastern Montana, describes hosting Young Man Afraid of His Horses during one of his cross-country journeys, observing "[h]e was old and undersized, yet his bearing was dignified and he looked very much a chief." He makes a gesture of sharing some of his hair with Alderson, a signifier of his status and generosity: "Young-Man-Afraid-of-His-Horses pulled his braided hair to the front, singled out a wisp of, I'm sure, not over a dozen hairs, and asked Mary to cut it off and give it to me. I had to be content and was profuse in my thanks."

Writing in the year of Montana's statehood, and just two years before the Wounded Knee Massacre on his home reservation of Pine Ridge, Young Man Afraid of His Horses reveals an emerging strategy for dealing with loss among the nations of the northern plains: cooperation across boundaries of former enmity. Ironically, the increasingly draconian reservation system removes the sources of conflict among tribal nations, for they no longer compete for control of prime hunting lands, nor seek honor through war coups and horse stealing. Lines of communication and friendship established tentatively, occasionally in the years of Lakota and Crow conflict now become lifelines, a means to share information, discuss the will and practices of the Americans, plan strategies of resistance or negotiation.

There is much to discuss for tribal leaders, for the Americans have moved with ruthless, if uneven, efficiency to reduce the nations' lands so that they can run more cattle, grow more crops, plant more towns, mine more minerals, take more trees, make more money. All the energies of the Gilded Age United States have been cut loose on the northern plains, all that commitment to incorporating this remote prairie into the economic web extending from Minneapolis, Chicago, New York, and London. This very year, 1889, will see a radical reduction of the Great Sioux Reservation in the Dakotas, easing white access to the Black Hills and confining the Sioux to ever smaller parcels of land, often unfit for the kind of agrarian life the Americans preach.

Reservation officials both on the ground and in Washington, D. C., fear the movement of Indians from reservation to reservation, suspicious of motive and impact. D. O. Cowen, agent at Fort Peck, writes with evident pique, "In the summer season of the year many of these Indians are inclined to wander about and steal off the reservation, notwithstanding the precautionary measures to prevent their nomadic freaks." Officials are especially concerned about provocative leaders such as Sitting Bull, who had visited the Crows in September 1886, and encouraged resistance to civilizing tactics. Sitting Bull's pretext for spending time with his former enemies was a return to the scene of his greatest military victory, the triumph over Custer at the Battle of the Little Bighorn ten years earlier. The Lakota leader was blunt in his assessment of the relative benefits of resisting or accommodating the Americans:

> See how the white men treat us and how they treat you. We get one and one half pounds of beef per ration, while you receive but one half pound. You are kept at home and made to work like slaves, while we do no labor and are permitted to ride from agency to agency and enjoy ourselves.

The Hunkpapa medicine man lingered two weeks on the Little Bighorn, preaching the imminent danger of allotment, a system he feared would steal Indian land. (The Dawes Severalty Act of 1887, also known as the General Allotment Act, would in fact require Indians to take up 160-acre homestead parcels, allowing the government to sell those homesteads not claimed by members of Indian nations.) Among those who listened intently to Sitting Bull's message was Deaf Bull, a Crow leader who played an important role in Sword Bearer's resistance in the fall of 1887, and who would not be released from imprisonment for that resistance until August of 1889.

As for Young Man Afraid of His Horses, though he is not granted permission to visit his Crow relatives in 1889, he will journey to see them in 1890, when he will encourage them to resist surrendering land to the emigrants. He will arrive with twenty Lakota just a few weeks before the Wounded Knee catastrophe. The Crow are under pressure to sell two million acres of their land on the western end of their reservation. Young Man Afraid of His Horses will share the bitterness and loss of the prior year's destruction of the Great Sioux Reservation, encouraging Plenty Coups and Pretty Eagle to oppose the initial terms for the land sale. The Crow agent also suspects Young Man Afraid of His Horses preaches the Messiah Craze, though in reality, the Lakota man stands in opposition to the Ghost Dance. Not surprisingly, then, that same agent will insist that Young Man Afraid of His Horses and his fellow Lakota leave the Crow Reservation. The land sale will go forward, though on better terms for the Crow people, and Young Man Afraid of His Horses will return to visit his relatives and allies the next year, and the year after that.

ON THE SIXTH DAY OF THE FIRST MONTH OF THE YEAR OF Montana's statehood, Marcus Daly writes to Samuel Hauser, "to tell you the truth I am so disappointed and so disgusted that I have now quit politics for good." What would lead this mining magnate, Irish immigrant, and prominent Democrat to write such a

Marcus Daly, 1895. Montana Historical Society Research Center Photograph Archives, Helena, Montana

weary, despairing sentence? Daly has just emerged from a bruis-
ing battle over election of Montana's final territorial delegate to
Congress. Having helped engineer the defeat of another mining
giant, William Andrews Clark, Daly finds himself debating the
worth of such poisonous efforts.

Daly's life embodies the magic of the American dream, the
political machinations of the Gilded Age, and the intense efforts
to remake Montana all in one. Yet he remains elusive, for his
family will destroy most of his private letters and papers upon
his death, and those who know him well will remain circum-
spect, cautious when discussing him. In Montana's mythology,
he will come down as the genial Irish foil to the surly, overtly
ambitious Clark, the Abel to Clark's Cain. Yet Daly left behind
an extraordinarily dense set of institutions, communities, and
companies that will provide evidence of things unseen. He is a
man of extraordinary reach whose determined efforts to build
out his Anaconda Mining Company stretched all across the
state of his adoption, extending to the forests of western Montana, the coal mines of north-central and south-central Montana (Belt and Red Lodge), the power sources of the Missouri
River at Great Falls, the points west and east reachable by the
railroad lines he helped build, and, of course, the towns of Butte
and Anaconda that he created by dint of will, capital, and a bot-
tomless self-regard.

Daly's life can exemplify the promise of his adopted country.
Born into poverty in Ireland, he fled the chaos and viciousness
of the Irish potato famine for New York in 1856 at the age of 15.
After working the usual odd jobs of a young, ill-educated immigrant, he crossed the continent to San Francisco via the isthmus
of Panama. He found his way to the Comstock Lode in Nevada,
there to learn the ins and outs of hard-rock silver mining and to
make the acquaintance of Samuel Clemens, who would later pen
one of the most effective takedowns ever in his description of a
corrupt William Andrews Clark. His adventures in Nevada led

to Utah, employment by the rich and ambitious Walker brothers, and finally the move north that defines his legacy: Daly arrived in Butte in 1876 at the behest of the Walkers to study up on the silver mines in this underdeveloped, still-remote part of the nation. Over the next twenty-four years, he will help transform this new-found land into a major industrial complex and a financial colossus through innate intelligence, mining savvy, outside capital, and shifting alliances with men named Haggin, Hearst, Hauser, Hammond, Hill, Billings, and more. He is a man born at the right moment, one who would know how to put the lax principles and large-scale capitalist transactions of the post-Civil War years to his use.

Yet moving closer to the man, to his actions, to his choices, a twenty-first century observer sees how his life embodies the chanciness and sheer luck of the ultra-wealthy. Take the origin of his legendary Anaconda Copper Company. He purchased the original Anaconda mine from another Irishman, Michael Hickey, in 1880. Hickey so named the mine because as a loyal Unionist he wanted to memorialize Grant's Grand Army of the Republic that surrounded Lee's army like an anaconda snake. Though Daly acquired the mine for its promising silver lodes, he soon discoverered massive copper veins that point to wealth on a scale hardly glimpsed to this stage of his life. In a nation soon dependent on this malleable metal ideal for electrical wires, Daly had just uncovered the resource that will justify calling Butte "the Richest Hill on Earth." Coy and avaricious, Daly secured the backing of California capitalists George Hearst, J. B. Haggin, and Lloyd Tevis to purchase adjoining properties, concealing as best he can the discovery of copper. He will close the Anaconda for a time to obscure his motives. Then, when the time is right, the market ready, he will re-open the mine and begin extracting and refining copper on a scale that will make Daly and Butte a national, even international, force. Once he sets this copper boom in motion, he will move purposefully to secure

Butte, Montana circa 1890-1895, corner of Park and Main, looking north on Main. Montana Historical Society Research Center Photograph Archives, Helena, Montana

the resources to feed the Anaconda's greedy maw: timber, coal, water, laborers. Daly will be portrayed as a one-time miner who had the common touch with his many hard-working miners; he will be renowned for his special commitment to employing Irish immigrants cut out of the same cloth as himself. Still, he amasses wealth at the expense of those very workers, operating on an implicit hierarchical principle that the strongest dominate and the weakest serve. He will employ spies and infiltrators of the mining and railroad worker unions to manage that most significant if at times intractable resource.

The year 1888 marked the moment when the personality differences, competition, and raw ambition of Daly and Clark, the Scotch-Irish business genius, fussy, meticulous, and effective, came to a head. Clark, ever desirous of political office, for him the cynosure of status, put himself forward as the Democratic candidate for Montana Territory's last non-voting representative to Congress, surely the prelude to becoming one of the new state's first senators. For all their differences, Clark and Daly were diehard Democrats, so surely Clark should have carried the day in a predominantly Democratic territory. But that's not what happened. Instead, the relative nonentity who ran on the Republican side, Thomas Carter, won a decisive victory.

Clark knew a terrible betrayal, a dark plot on the part of Daly and his faction, must have accounted for this unimaginable outcome: "The conspiracy was a gigantic one, well planned, and well carried out, even though it did involve the violation of some of the most sacred confidences. . . . However as you suggest the day of retribution may come when treason may be considered odious." Election results from Butte and the western counties dominated by the timber industry told the tale: Overwhelming support for a Republican, almost unheard of in this territory that had so long held out against the Republican primacy of the federal government. Surely, Daly and his henchmen had

ordered miners and loggers to side with a party that did not hold
their concerns, their hopes dear.

Since Daly so carefully concealed his handiwork and his motives, Montanans have been left to speculate about the source of
this upset. Some will claim Clark the banker betrayed Daly when
the immigrant sought to purchase the Alice mine in 1876, and
so the Irish American had simply bided his time to exact a most
precise and telling revenge. Others will point to Clark's condescending comments about Daly's partner Haggin, of Turkish
extraction and dark-skinned, whom Clark may have dismissed
with an odious epithet. Others wonder if the vote rigging re-
sulted from that classic, tragic Irish conflict between the Catholic south and the Protestant north (Daly is a devout Catholic,
while Clark, true to his Ulster roots, adheres to the Presbyterian
faith). Yet an economic motive seems the most likely cause of
this subterfuge, for Daly, in alliance with the Missoula businessman A. B. Hammond, has formed the Montana Improvement
Company, which has been harvesting vast quantities of timber from federal lands to feed his mines, smelters, and railroad
lines. The Democratic administration of Grover Cleveland has
brought suit against this timber conglomerate. The election of
a Republican president in 1888, more hoped for than fully believed in, could mean a reversal of fortune, for Benjamin Harrison's party promises far less scrutiny of such dicey use of the
public domain. In the event of Harrison's victory, a Republican
representative might prove the antidote to ominous legal action
against Daly.

Whatever the true source of the betrayal, and all of these
causes may have played a part, Daly, no seeker of public office
and often impatient with the art and corruption of politics, has
had his fill for the time being. Yet his despairing letter to Hauser
will stand as a brief pause, a moment of doubt, rather than a
statement of principle. Many political battles lie ahead for these

two Copper Kings, most notoriously the buying of the state capital in 1894.

PRESTON H. LESLIE, PENULTIMATE GOVERNOR OF MONTANA Territory, charges the newly seated legislature with the solemn task of preparing Montana for statehood:

> At this crisis in our history, when we expect soon to assume the dignity and responsibilities of statehood, your position becomes more responsible and more honored than any of your predecessors; in no small degree your labors may aid in laying broad and deep the foundations of the coming commonwealth of Montana. Spanning nearly five degrees of latitude and twelve of longitude, interspersed by vast mountain chains, Montana will serve as the connecting link between the Pacific and central states, with the Atlantic states so closely allied, making one indestructible union. Our mountains veined with gold and silver and the more useful metals, our placers filled with gold, and wide prairies covered with grasses, are fast giving us individual and public wealth. To secure the greatest prosperity in these vast industries will require your best thought and ripest statesmanship.

Governor Leslie proffers a vision of the territory as the essential link binding the nation, as though regressing, briefly, to the very conflict that gave birth to Montana in 1864, the War of the Rebellion or War of Northern Aggression. The fierce struggle between Republicans and Democrats at the territory's founding, fully revealed in Governor Sidney Edgerton's vexed speech to the first territorial legislature, has endured these twenty-five years through often vicious political infighting between determined Republicans such as Wilbur Fisk Sandersand unrepentant Democrats such as Samuel Hauser. No wonder Leslie anxiously asserts Montana serves to assure the United States are indeed "one indestructible union."

Leslie sketches in broad strokes the dominant industries of the emerging state: mining in western and central Montana and running livestock on the central and eastern plains. His reference to "ripest statesmanship" hints at the ongoing tensions between these "vast industries," for ranching and mining interests have long been at odds over issues such as taxation of mines (not surprisingly, mine owners insist only the metals extracted be taxed rather than the full mining properties), railroads (the Northern Pacific Railroad's vast lands, granted by the federal government in 1864, offer opportunities to miners and ranchers alike), and control of water sources.

The address that follows this almost visionary preamble is dry in many senses. Leslie, a tall, dignified former governor of Kentucky, and a loyal Democrat appointed by the Cleveland administration, is an avowed temperance man who begins by urging passage of anti-drinking laws. He then turns bureaucratic, sticking closely to the more prosaic realities of governance, focusing on creation of foundational civil institutions such as public schools, a penitentiary, a house of reform for youth, an insane asylum, and a state library. Though he briefly returns to near-eloquence when describing an agrarian vision for Montana, he concludes by assuring his auditors (and perhaps himself) that though a vast territory of competing economic and cultural interests, Montana is one whole, a unified almost-state. A political appointee with few ties to Montana Territory, and one who has been effectively marginalized by such prominent businessmen as Daly, Clark, Hauser, and Charles Broadwater of Helena, Leslie may well have decided to avoid the major controversies implied by his opening. He is also aware his time as governor is fast coming to an end, for with the election of Republican Benjamin Harrison to the presidency, Leslie will step down to make way for the new president's appointee.

Yet even granting the governor's understandable caution, one omission bears notice: Leslie refers once, briefly, to the Indian nations that had called this region home long before the emigrants arrived: "It is almost twenty-five years since the few white men and women then in Montana, surrounded by many unfriendly Indians, decided to plant permanently in these mountains the standard of American civilization." At the end of the decade that saw the reduction of the Blackfeet Reserve north of the Missouri River to three constricted reservations, the decade that saw the creation of the Tongue River or Northern Cheyenne Reservation by executive order in 1884, the decade that saw steady erosion of Crow lands by ranchers, miners, and railroads, the decade that will see the final surrender of Salish chief Charlo to the necessity of moving from the Bitterroot to the Flathead valley, Montana Territory's governor sees no need to acknowledge an enduring native presence. Perhaps once again Leslie sidesteps controversy, or perhaps that silence speaks volumes about the settler community's view of those original inhabitants: out of sight, out of mind, and ultimately erased from Montana's future.

The constitution that emerges in August of 1889 enabling Montana "to assume the dignity and responsibilities of statehood" will favor stock-growing and mining interests. Of course that founding document will not be the first so conceived. The legendary Thomas Francis Meagher led an ill-fated attempt to jumpstart statehood by convening a constitutional convention in 1866, just two years after the territory's formation. The effort was so poorly organized that the draft constitution has not survived the test of time—the only copy was apparently lost on the way to the printer. A more promising effort took place in 1884 as Montanans read the tea leaves of national will—since a Democratic president had been elected for the first time since the Civil War in the person of Grover Cleveland, hopes rose that Montana might at last become a state. Such was not to be, for

Congress remained in the hands of a Republican Party not eager
to grant full voting power in Congress and the presidential election to a manifestly Democratic territory.

The 1889 constitutional delegates lean heavily on the document drafted in 1884. None other than William Andrews Clark
chairs the convention, and prominent ranchers such as Conrad
Kohrs are active participants in the deliberations. Fully one half
of the delegates are linked to the mining industry. The founders create a cumbersome executive branch with twenty depart-
ments, perhaps overreacting to a sense that Montana citizens'
interests have been neglected during the territorial days. That
executive branch will metastasize, creating an unwieldy "head"
to state government that will prompt a new constitutional convention in 1972. Not surprisingly, the convention finds itself
most sharply divided over how to apportion political power in
the legislative branch among counties east and west. The familiar Montana divide between competing cultural regions, created
by the odd combination of mountain valleys and high plains at
the territory's birth, emerges in battles over how many representatives and senators each county can claim. By apportioning one
senator to every county, the founders grant the predominantly
agricultural eastern region outsized clout. The Constitution
also limits the legislature to 60 days, assuring hasty and often
ill-informed deliberation. On that most fundamental matter of
all, the right to vote, the state constitution recognizes all male
citizens over 21 years of age, regardless of race or creed. One of
the most contested and passionate efforts of all during the convention, granting women suffrage, goes down to defeat on a surprisingly close vote. Montana women are a powerful presence
at the state's founding and will remain so throughout Montana's
relatively short history.

Senator William A. Clark, President, Constitutional Conventions, 1884 and 1889. MONTANA HISTORICAL SOCIETY RESEARCH CENTER PHOTO-GRAPH ARCHIVES, HELENA, MONTANA

FEBRUARY

In which Louis Riel's case rises to the surface, Kim Poo is shot dead, the Knights of Pythias celebrate an important anniversary, and President Cleveland signs the Enabling Legislation for Montana statehood.

———

Alderman Bullard returned yesterday from a hurried trip to the camp at Red Lodge and reports considerable bustle and activity there over the advent of the railroad. The track is now within fifteen miles of Red Lodge and plenty of iron and ties to get there with. . . . There are now about one hundred and twenty-five men employed in the coal mines and more are hired as fast as they make application. . . . Mr. Bullard thinks there will be quite a rush to the camp from this out and that it will be a lively place.

———

SIR: I AM IN THE PAINFUL CONDITION OF BEING BROUGHT before the court at Regina, under charge of high treason.

I have the honor to let you know, to inform you that I am not guilty. I have the highest respect for the stipendiary magistrates before whom I have to answer; but their court is not the one to try my case, as that case had its origin long before the stipendiary court of Regina existed.

As [an] American citizen, I humbly appeal to the Government of my adopted land for help through you. I assure you my request is not inspired by any of those feelings which might have a tendency to create difficulty between the United States and England.

I am small, and my humble condition prevents me from being heard by the British dignitaries of the Dominion. I am confident that if you would deign write to the American Government in my behalf, they would not refuse to say a good word in my favor; that good word would secure me a fair trial, and a fair trial would save me.

While in Montana, I have exerted myself to be a good citizen, and I have worked in harmony with the United States authorities in the Territory. I have even had the honor to be appointed several times United States special deputy marshal. If I mistake not there are in the Department of Justice at Washington documents which speak favorably of me.

In God I trust that a friendly word to the British minister would go far to protect me from inattention.

Also, I have no means to defray the expenses of a trial such as the one I have to stand. I beg the American Government to help me that way too. Please transmit my humble petition, if it is not altogether out of place.

Thanking you for all the favors you have done me in the past, and praying that you may be fully rewarded, I hope the Providence of God will spare me, through as generous a consul as you, and through as good a Government as that of the States.

I have the honor to be, very respectfully, your humble servant, LOUIS RIEL

Louis Riel. SASKATCHEWAN ARCHIVES BOARD

So wrote a visionary, believer, and disheartened leader of a quest to create a Métis nation in the heart of the continent in 1885. Riel pleaded with the American consul to Winnipeg to protect him from Canadian justice, for he was about to stand trial on the charge of treason by the government north of the Medicine Line. He chose his audience well, for James Wickes Taylor had long been an advocate for American annexation of the Canadian plains, and he and Riel knew each other. The proud Métis had come down out of the north to live for a time in Montana, seeking sanctuary, but that proved a temporary stay. He returned to his beloved Canadian prairies to lead a failed resistance.

Riel rises to the surface once more in 1889, for on February 11, the Senate asks the elected president, Benjamin Harrison, to share all documents speaking to whether Riel in fact had been an American citizen at the time of his execution in November 1885, one who had been unjustly tried and hanged by the Canadians. The president sends the Senate the complete dossier of pleas and government replies on March 11, just seven days after his inauguration. That collection of documents discloses the supplicant's justification and fear and the U. S. government's mixed sympathy and indifference. It offers uncanny access to the thinking of an often misunderstood, mysterious figure out of Montana's past. Riel's story provides another crucial link in the making of Montana, for his life and death summon the wanderings of his people, the Métis, the mixed-blood descendants of French emigrants and Indian women, and the travails of the Chippewa and Cree people who had lived on both sides of the Medicine Line and became known as the Landless Indians in Montana following the 1885 resistance.

Riel was a child of an elite Métis family in the Red River Valley of what is now Manitoba. The oldest of eleven, since he showed precocious intelligence and a burning passion for knowledge, he received a superb education in Quebec. When he returned to his homeland in 1868 at the age of 24, he was immediately plunged into a struggle for sovereignty and survival for his people. At long last the Dominion of Canada had cast its eyes upon the western plains, despite the daunting distances from Ontario to Rupert's Land (essentially the territory today covered by Canada's western provinces). The United States also coveted that country, imagining one solid landmass stretching from the border territories and states to Alaska.

Riel, gifted orator, poet, and occasional visionary, assumed leadership of the Métis resistance to Anglo-Protestant control of his homeland. Showing impressive foresight, he declared a provisional government in the briefly ungoverned territory. The Hudson Bay Company was in the process of selling Rupert's Land to the Dominion, but since the transaction had not yet been completed, the Red River country could be seen as a political vacuum. Riel and his people drafted a Bill of Rights echoing the American version, and in the end the Dominion negotiated creation of the Province of Manitoba, seemingly assuring Métis rights to property and political freedom. Riel had clearly sided with Canadian claims on the plains, though he would later attempt to reignite American ambitions for control when he was seeking escape from execution.

Had events ended there, Riel might have claimed a major political victory and settled down to life as esteemed leader and patriarch. But he and his fellow Métis put to death Thomas Scott, one of the most voluble, insulting, and defiant of "Orangemen" (those with strong Protestant leanings who objected to Catholic sway in the new province). Scott's execution as the resistance was coming to an end placed the mark of Cain upon Riel. The British-oriented settlers and politicians who moved into Manitoba would not forgive or forget this "martyrdom." Many of Riel's associates were hunted down and murdered, and Riel himself barely escaped vengeance.

Riel entered upon a peripatetic, restless, unsatisfying life as exile, spending time in the States, being elected to the Dominion Parliament twice, only to be expelled, and being confined for a time to an insane asylum, diagnosed with megalomania and delusions. Riel's story repeatedly raises questions about the difference between madness and political genius, between vision and delusion. Was he a prescient political thinker who had the courage to follow his convictions, or was he a madman caught up in deceptive dreams that cost him and his people? He at last migrated to Montana in 1879, drawn to the traditional Métis hunting camps along the Milk River. He and his compatriots were forced by American troops to relocate to Spring Creek in the Judith Mountains, and so they became a fixture in the Lewistown area. He joined his fate to a Métis woman, Marguerite, a marriage that seemed to provide a degree of contentment. No doubt seeking economic security and a steady home for his young family, he then took up the life of schoolteacher at St. Peter's Mission south of the Sun River. One witness observed, "The work was monotonous and elementary but he seemed to enjoy it, and satisfied his employers except when he talked politics which made them impatient, or when he discussed religion as he did occasionally which gave them alarm. He pleased the parents of the pupils and carried with him until he died various letters of appreciation which he received while he was a teacher."

This sympathetic observer alludes to Riel's active involvement in Montana and tribal politics. In a remarkably bold and visionary move during his time in the Milk River country, he had attempted to unify the Blackfeet, Assiniboine, Cree, and Hunkpapa Sioux under Sitting Bull in a single nation along the American/Canadian border. While Montanans aspired to secure their place in the United States by achieving statehood, Riel envisioned an entirely new nation, carving out a large swath of the northern Great Plains for peoples related by blood, culture, and belief. Rebuffed by Indian leaders who did not know or trust him, he turned to advocating for a joint reservation in Montana serving as home for the Chippewa, Cree, and Métis. When that effort also failed, Riel focused on more prosaic political goals, enlisting his Métis compatriots to vote for the Republican nominee for territorial representative, aggressively promoting the interests of the party that expressed deeper commitment to native justice than the still-dominant Democratic Party. The Métis leader landed in jail, accused of election fraud for encouraging "ineligible" mixed-raced people to vote, a charge that was summarily dismissed. He seems also to have communicated unorthodox religious views that exceeded the patience of his Jesuit hosts at St. Peter's. Those views have been the source of controversy down to the present day, for when put on trial for what he was about to do in Saskatchewan, his lawyers argued he was driven to resistance by insanity, as evidenced by those very prophecies. Riel adamantly denied these claims of insanity, undermining his defense but preserving his self-respect and forever complicating historians' understanding of his life and behavior.

On June 4, 1884, Riel received four visitors at St. Peter's Mission, most famously, Gabriel Dumont, renowned buffalo hunter and leader of men. The visitors carried news that the people of the Red River carts were under duress in the emerging province of Saskatchewan, subject to many of the same abuses suffered in 1869-70. They appealed to Riel to return to serve as counselor, putting to use his knowledge and experience from the Manitoba years. This request seemed fulfillment of Riel's vision of himself as "prophet," guiding creation of an independent province ruled by members of many races and ethnicities on the plains of Canada. He also desired to claim land still owed him from the settlement of 1870.

Passing through Sun River, the delegation stopped to visit with the editor of the local paper, who noted, "Mr. Riel says that he is an American citizen, and that he considers the land over which the stars and stripes wave his home, and now only goes to

assist his people as much as lays in his power, and after which—
be it much or little— he will return to Montana." Ominously, the
newspaper editor also shared the story of his serving as drum-
mer boy during the unrest in the Red River country, a time during which he desired Riel's death, largely for the execution of
Thomas Scott. Clearly, that rash act lingered in the collective
memory of the region, an important fact when Riel faced trial
in just over a year from the day he passed through Sun River.
Despite his declared desire to return to Montana, he never set
foot in the territory again.

Riel put the lessons of Manitoba to work in Saskatchewan.
If anything, he showed more political skill, collaborating with
his many Métis, white, and mixed-race English and Indian supporters to draft a petition for just treatment of settlers who had
risked so much to claim land in the West. When that petition
brought no results, Riel and Dumont openly threatened armed
resistance, apparently more an intimidation tactic than a sincere commitment to violence. But as so often happens in highly
charged, confusing circumstances, awkward encounters and
unintended deaths led to Louis Riel's surrender to Canadian
authorities. Ironically, his friend and partner, Gabriel Dumont,
came to resent Riel's refusal to wage an effective guerilla campaign, preventing Dumont from using tactics such as aggressive
attack following a battle or full-bore ambush. Riel's heart did not
seem to be in the fight, only in the cause.

Riel's role as revolutionary was rendered even more controversial by his religious beliefs, for he imagined replacing the
Catholic Church, so central to Métis life, with a New World religion modeled on the Church but looking more like a Protestant
sect. This original creed reveals that this gifted, melancholic,
unsteady man was dreaming of a far more profound revolution than might be apparent at first glance. He was imagining
a mixed-race polity that practiced an original form of religion,
all rooted in the place, the traditions, and the values of indig-

enous peoples and settlers. But those visions also point back to his confinement in an insane asylum. His insistence on being called Louis "David" Riel, highlighting his strong connection to the Biblical king who slew Goliath, only compounds these concerns.

Riel surrendered to Dominion authorities on the belief his arrest would divert them from punishing the Métis, an assumption that proved somewhat accurate. He also believed he would be found not guilty once his plea for justice was made. That assumption showed his naivete and his lack of understanding of the larger political and social forces at work on the northern plains. The Anglo-Protestant majority had long coveted his punishment for Thomas Scott's execution. Riel's boundary-defying plans to join diverse nations, Indian and white, in new political units threatened both the American and Canadian national projects. His attorneys' efforts to prove he was innocent by reason of insanity foundered badly (in large part because Riel argued vehemently against it in court), and he was sentenced to death. During appeals of that verdict, Riel managed to smuggle a message to Grover Cleveland setting forth his people's grievances and encouraging U.S. annexation of Saskatchewan. That message became part of the dossier released to the United States Senate by President Harrison in 1889:

> That the Hudson's Bay Company endeavoured . . . to hand over to the invaders that government of the Northwest which England had so constantly neglected and so obstinately kept at the disposal of trading adventurers. . . . The undersigned, your humble petitioner, submits and respectfully claims that by committing this other remarkable series of outrages against the Northwest, the British Government have again forfeited all title and right of governing it; [y]our humble petitioner submits that the people of the Northwest, left to themselves, had to orga-

nize and to constitute a state of their own, to take care of
public affairs, and for their protection. . . . Consequently
the British government has had neither the right of intro-
ducing the confederation in the Northwest, as they did
in 1870, neither the right to maintaining it there since.
. . . Before God and before men, the undersigned, your
humble petitioner, declares his native land free, and has
the honor to ask your excellency and most honorable
ministers for the advantage of annexing the Northwest to
the great American Republic. . . . Your humble petitioner
respectfully asks, as American citizen, for your kind and
powerful protection.

Given his imminent death, this appeal may seem disingenuous—was Riel committed to American control of Saskatchewan,
or was this a ploy to gain a temporary reprieve from execution?
Compounding the historian's questions are Riel's words written
just a few months earlier, "I used to live wretchedly in the United
States among serpents, amid poisonous vipers. . . . The United
States are hell for an honest man. . . . Oh, what a great misfor-
tune it is to be obliged to seek refuge in the United States."

Riel's pleas and appeals failed; he was hanged on November
16, 1885. That murderous act hovers over Canadian history, for
Riel gathers to himself a multitude of meanings: advocate for indigenous rights, Western independence, French Canadian and
Catholic sovereignty, the right to governance by the people, and
so much more. That death also hovers over Montana history,
since Riel's resistance set loose the many allies who had fought
with him, especially the Métis, Cree, and Chippewa.

Gabriel Dumont fled from arrest by riding hard to Fort
Assinniboine near present-day Havre, only to be arrested as a
dangerous insurgent. He was ordered released, allowing him to
live with his Métis relatives in Montana while ruminating on the
sad denouement of a messy, compelling, failed act of defiance.

He represents the many Métis supporters of the resistance who become displaced in the Milk River and Spring Creek regions. A group of Crees and Chippewas under the leadership of Little Bear and Rocky Boy, numbering 137 men, women, and children, journeyed to the Montana plains as well, revisiting ground familiar to them from their migrations south of the Medicine Line to hunt buffalo and visit their relatives. Little Bear had led his people in an attack against the Canadians at Frog Lake during the resistance, resulting in the death of nine enemies, hence his flight to Montana. (His father Big Bear would be unjustly convicted of murder and suffer two years in prison, only to die shortly after his release.) These dispossessed Chippewa and Cree were detained as well when they entered the territory, but when Canadian authorities did not request their extradition, they found themselves living on the margins of reservations and towns. They became a pawn between the U.S. and Canadian governments, recognized by neither and so ensnared by the in-between zone where they received neither land nor supplies. Riel's foresight to imagine a joint reservation now took on even more meaning.

The landless Indians are very much on the minds of Montana leaders as they set about creating a state. Newspapers report on their whereabouts, their habits, their seeming danger: "Soon after the Reil [sic] rebellion was crushed out in 1885, about 150 Cree Indians, who had been identified with the rebellion, came over the line and established themselves at various Indian agencies in northern Montana, but more particularly around Fort Assinaboine [sic]. . . . The question of feeding them has been a source of much annoyance to the Indian bureau. On several occasions it has drawn the attention of congress to the necessities of these Indians, but no appropriation has ever been made for them." For the settler culture, the non-treaty people appear a threat to transplanted customs and established routines.

An article from the *Fort Benton River Press* dated June 26, 1889 communicates similar concerns:

> We have in Northern and Western Montana a nomadic people who recognize no government as theirs and acknowledge no tribal relations. They know no home save the wide rolling prairie, and it matters little to them, apparently, so they have a little to eat and much to drink. We refer to the roaming half-breeds, wherever they hail from, whether from the British or the American side of the line. . . . Let it be remembered that we are speaking of the roving half-breeds; those in whom the Indian nature seems to pre-dominate; those who will not settle down on land allowed them by either government, and who wander blither and yon at their own sweet will, living from hand to mouth, and spending their time in frivolous pursuits and dissipation. As long as northern Montana was a vast Indian reservation, and game was plenty, it mattered little how far or how much they wandered or how improvident they were. But the time has come when this government, or both the Canadian and United States' governments should each take their share of these people and provide some means to keep them within bounds and see that they cease their present mode of life. Wandering around in bands as they do, they are a constant terror to isolated settlers and a menace to good order generally.

While the writer specifically attacks the Métis, he reveals the reigning attitudes toward all displaced Indians. These "boundless" people frighten the writer by their refusal to stay in place, to conform to American norms. There's more than a hint of envy for their "frivolous pursuits and dissipation," a sense they're playing while the sober-sided writer works hard. The article casts the mind back to Johnny Grant, the early emigrant to the Deer Lodge Valley who became known as the host of free-spirited Métis and French Canadian visitors during the 1860s. Even Granville Stuart waxed eloquent about the fun to be had at one of Johnny's mid-winter dances in 1862. Grant left Montana in the late 1860s, in part because he struggled to pay taxes on his property, in larger part because his mix-raced marriages and playful life proved anathema to many setters drawn to the territory by gold, merchant, and farming prospects. In a sense the article's writer has reproduced the harsh judgments of the British Canadian agents who were so offended by Louis Riel's dreams that they put him to death. A new orthodoxy has taken root in Montana.

As for the landless Indians, their struggles are only beginning in 1889. It would not be until 1916 that the Rocky Boy Reservation would be established on the Hi-Line to provide a home for the Chippewa-Cree people. The Little Shell people, descendants of those tribal members who inhabited both sides of the Canadian border, remain an unrecognized nation to this day.

As I entered the cabin I had no intention of killing the Chinaman and did not do so until I was obliged to, in order to save my own life. I made my way through the front room to the opium den, my revolver remained in my belt. When I got into the den I found several Chinamen smoking pipes, and some more were lying down and did not seem to realize anything that transpired. I made an effort to seize a pipe from one of the men, when they all rushed for me. Then I drew my revolver and fired into the bunch of them, and heard one scream immediately after the shot. They crowded in on me then, and tried to get the weapon from me. I then called to Opp to come in, and as soon as he came to my rescue, they also tried to get his gun, and he also fired once, but which of the two shots killed Kim Poo I could not tell.

A raid on an opium den in the remote mining town of Granite goes terribly wrong. An inexperienced "deputy" of uncertain name (Carroll? Fretwell?) is told to enter the den at night, since he will not be suspected of being an officer of the law, and if he spots a pipe in use, make an arrest. This quondam deputy panics and fires twice, randomly, shattering the leg of one man and killing another.

The man dead at the scene had been a well-respected citizen of the Territory: "Kim Poo . . . is said to have been a very intelligent celestial, quite prominent as a leader and adviser among his countrymen. He was a past master of a Chinese Masonic lodge and was much smarter than the average of his race." That final clause carries a world of meaning for Montana in 1889. The Chinese form a critical part of the Territory's population in the 1880s and 90s (the census of 1890 shows a peak population of 2,532 out of a total population of 142,924). They create especially vibrant communities in Butte, Helena, Missoula, and Fort Benton. Yet Montanans hold little regard for a people so vital to the region's well-being.

Driven from their homeland by war and poverty, they mine, open restaurants, operate laundries, and, perhaps most importantly from the locals' point of view, build the railroads that connect Montana to the major market centers east and west. Their working lives are often shockingly difficult: "[Overcoming nature's] insurmountable barrier . . . cable ropes holding a plank staging go down the precipitous sides of the mountain. Down the rope ladders, to this staging clamber Chinamen armed with drills, and soon the rock sides are filled with Giant powder. Then they clamber up, the blast is fired, and the foothold made by the explosive soon swarms with Celestials; the 'can't be done' has been done. . ." Though paid $.50 an hour less than Euro-American laborers, as many as 10,000 Chinese joined "Hallett's Army," the mixed-race team laying the Northern Pacific Railroad track from Idaho to Montana. Their living conditions were unsanitary and dangerous, and many of them died from such gruesome acts as a misdirected dynamite blast that sent rock shrapnel through a campsite. One newspaper estimated that 1,000 Chinese died during the laying of the track, but that estimate surely understates the toll taken. As the reporter ruefully remarked, "verily the road was built with Chinaman's bones."

Despite the important role they play in Montana's economy, the Chinese face steady, unyielding prejudice. The year 1881 saw passage of the Opium Act banning use of the substance by the Montana Territorial Legislature, the very act that led to Kim Poo's senseless death. Montana's anti-opium smoking law reveals how drug prohibitions hew to cultural prejudices, for the act was designed to prevent Chinese use of a substance that was taken up readily enough by Americans in the form of laudanum, a popular form of "medicine" at the time. In fact, opium as smoked seems to have been much less harmful than the stout alcohol consumed by many Montanans. The drug also helped shield the user from the pain and suffering, mental and physical, caused by occupations such as railroad worker and miner.

Passage of the law followed increasing use by whites, raising the specter of contamination of the host culture by an alien practice. While the law was supposedly meant to prevent use of a harmful substance, it was as much about encouraging the Chinese to leave Montana. These strangers in a strange land seemed beyond the pale, disturbing to the dominant culture, their hair, dress, and manners "barbaric," their speech unintelligible (and so presumably unintelligent): "The Chinaman's life is not our life; his religion is not our religion. His habits, superstitions, and modes of life are disgusting. He is a parasite, floating across the Pacific and thence penetrating into the interior towns and cities. . . ." Yet Chinese emigrants carried a sophisticated, adaptable, welcoming culture, their food, laundries, and labor filling crucial niches in a developing territory.

Even more devastating to the Chinese in Montana was the federal Exclusion Act of 1882, the first legislation designed to prevent immigration by a specific national group. The act blocked arrival of Chinese laborers for ten years and prevented naturalization by Chinese immigrants. It did, however, allow for the continued presence of those Chinese already in place in the United States. The law was justified as an attempt to preserve work for Americans in the topsy-turvy economic times of the 1880s (the U.S. weathered a terrible depression in 1873 and frequent recessions since). But as the Opium Act reveals, the roots of the law lie far deeper than that. Discrimination against this emigrant group only increased after passage of the Exclusion Act, as though that political act provided sanction for daily slights and outright acts of insult and resistance. Butte's mayor in 1882, William Owsley, featured the slogan, "Down with Chinese Cheap Labor."

In 1889, a charismatic, influential Chinese doctor, Huie Pock, arrives in Butte. He will have an extraordinary career as healer of ailments for Chinese and whites alike. A 1901 advertisement sets forth his skills with confidence and zest: "Dr. Huie Pock. 12 Years in Butte. Generation doctor of China from grandfather down. Born and schooled in the profession. Treats all diseases, making a specialty of chronic troubles. Consult me before you waste your life away." His fame will skyrocket after he provides a cure for William Clark's daughter. Yet he too faces cruel mistreatment and organized efforts to force him out of Butte. He will not be one to take that lying down, however—he will fight back in court and win. His store at 227 South Main Street will provide fancy Chinese and Japanese goods, as well as herbal remedies. During an 1896-97 boycott of Chinese businesses organized by white-only labor unions, supporters of the boycott will stand guard outside Pock's shop, warning off customers, leading to a sharp fall in sales. Pock's business faces a dire threat since he

Dr. Huie Pock, 1914. Montana Historical Society Research Center Photograph Archives, Helena, Montana

may not be able to pay his city business license. Pock joins a suit
against the boycotters, declaring in an affidavit,

> That by the concerted and joint action of the defendants
> and their confederates, he knows of the conspiracy and
> combination in the bill of complaint in this action set
> forth and described; that for the last three months and
> more, said defendants or some of them have been en-
> gaged in carrying or causing to be carried the banners
> and pictures, transparencies, mottoes and floats through
> the streets in the City of Butte aforesaid, in conspicuous
> and prominent places in the presence of large numbers
> of inhabitants thereof, and persons therein; that the same
> are defamatory and libelous of all persons of Chinese de-
> scent, and were so designed and intended to be done to
> excite the animosity of the citizens of said Butte towards
> the complainants in this action, and others of Chinese
> descent, and that they do so excite animosity and malice
> against persons of Chinese nativity and descent, and that
> certain of said defendants by the procurement of said
> defendants and others as affiants believe, have for the
> last three months, or thereabouts been standing, and yet
> continue to stand upon the side walk in front of, or in the
> immediate vicinity of divers and sundry places of busi-
> ness of the complainants and other Chinese, accosting the
> patrons of said Chinese, advising them that the said place
> of business of such Chinese are boycotted, and directing
> that they refrain from patronizing them.

Despite its legal formality, the affidavit gives voice to Huie
Pock's hurt, anger, and pride. None other than Wilbur Sanders,
the infamous prosecutor for the Vigilance Committee in the
1860s and a die-hard Republican ever since, represents the Chinese since he has little to lose—his politics cause him to challenge the Populists and silver advocates and so the labor unions

Wilbur Fisk Sanders walking down Main Street in Butte, Montana, past seated Indians, circa late 1800s. Montana Historical Society Research Center Photograph Archives, Helena, Montana

hold him in low regard. His defense will prove effective, for after three years, the complainants win a judgment in their favor.
Though the defendants are only ordered to pay the complainants' legal fees (which they subsequently refuse to do, claiming
bankruptcy), Pock and his fellow countrymen have won a signal
victory in their quest for recognition and respect. Yet in many
ways that victory will come too late—many Chinese businesses
will be forced to close.

In Miles City the Knights of Pythias celebrate the national organization's twenty-fifth anniversary on February 19
with a grand banquet. The local newspaper, while remaining
tactfully evasive about details of the event (appropriate since the
Knights maintain strict secrecy about their rituals), lauds the
organization as a noble effort by Americans to carry on a spirit
of fraternity and charity. The Knights of Pythias were created in
1864 to promote brotherhood and self-sacrifice at a moment of
deep violence and sectional hatred. In the words of "Sir Knight"
Whitney, keynote speaker at the banquet, "We are proud of our
order because it is an American institution; conceived in the
universality of brotherly friendship it was born at a time when
men and passions had been aroused by civil warfare, when
homes were desolate and brothers were warring against brothers. . . .Its lessons taught friendship first; then patriotism, love of
country and obedience to its laws." Whitney further observes,
rather grandly, "The recognized aim of all secret orders is to assist the life of a man's better nature."

But how did the order gain its curious name? Pythias, also
known as Phintias, was a citizen of ancient Syracuse who was
condemned to death for his opposition to the tyrant Dionysius.
His friend Damon offered himself up as collateral so that Pythias could journey to bid farewell to his family. On the day of
execution, since Pythias had not yet returned, Damon was led
to his execution, only to be startled and relieved when his friend

arrived just in time to spare him death. The tyrant was so moved by this display of friendship that he commuted Pythias's sentence. The story appealed to the order's founder, Justus Rathbone, as a compelling tale of selflessness and fraternity at the end of the bloody Civil War. Rathbone conceptualized a series of secret rituals based in part on his experience with the Masons to signal the members' ascent to various ranks, culminating with "Sir Knight." The order is open to white men of sound health—women and members of other races need not apply.

The Knights of Pythias are typical of the many fraternal orders that have taken root in Montana, the male counterparts to important female societies such as the Women's Christian Temperance Union. At a time when governments provide little in the way of protection against life's vicissitudes, the secret orders offer not just friendship and business contacts but health and life insurance, a hedge against uncertain fate. The orders also indulge a male taste for a fanciful return to medieval customs, rooted as they are in the masons' guilds of the late middle ages. Perhaps the secret rituals are as much as anything an opportunity to journey back, through imagination, to a seemingly simpler time, before advanced industrialization and suspect, complex financial dealings. No wonder Mark Twain feels inspired to publish *A Connecticut Yankee in King Arthur's Court* in 1889, a perplexing account of a Gilded Age American's journey to that mythical time. The most famous of fraternal orders was the Masons, often acknowledged as a key force behind the vigilanteeism of the 1860s, though in truth the secret order's role in those still-haunting events may have been exaggerated. Still, fully fifty per cent of the delegates to the 1889 Constitutional Convention are Masons. Male fraternal orders peak in membership and prestige in the late nineteenth and early twentieth centuries in the United States, signaling their importance, their appeal at a time of rapid change. In an era of social Darwinism and class conflict, such voluntary organizations must have served as a hedge against competitive pressures.

Perhaps no organization better represents that appeal than the Ancient Order of Hibernians, a Catholic association limited to those of Irish ancestry. The AOH thrives in Butte in the 1880s and 90s, since "[t]he copper mining city . . . was for its workforce a place of multiple horrors. Built on untimbered hills at an elevation of 5,000 to 6,500 feet, the city was described as looking like a 'gigantic ship wreck.'" Men of Irish birth and ancestry dominate the mining industry of the 1880s, in part because of Marcus Daly's prominent lead, in part because of the ready fit between Irish trained in hard rock mining and the emerging copper colossus. AOH serves these ethnic needs in a variety of ways: assuring work in the mines for members, providing sick and death benefits for laborers and their families, offering a dating service for lonely workers, even supplying nurses for the ailing. Given the high rate of mining accidents, injuries, and crippling lung diseases such as tuberculosis and silicosis, the order must seem a godsend in a frightening, unstable world. Yet AOH is rooted not just in labor needs for work, safety, and security but in the simmering nationalism of expats who hold an abiding scorn for the British. No wonder the Ancient Order of Hibernians will often be criticized for serving the needs of one ethnic enclave over and against those of so many emigrant groups, including those from central and northern Europe.

ON FEBRUARY 22 PRESIDENT CLEVELAND SIGNS THE ENABLING Legislation that sets the terms for Montana's becoming a state. After twenty-five years, the territory can at last claim majority status, an equality with the established states, a mature ability to shape the nation's future through voting members of Congress. Statehood will also free Montana to encourage foreign investment in industries such as mining. The legislation establishes conditions for admission, however, imparting a final paternalistic fillip to the territories.

Montana, acting in concert with Dakota Territory, to be split into North and South, and Washington, will elect 75 delegates to a constitutional convention. In the almost idealistic phrasing of the Act, "The constitutions shall be republican in form, and make no distinction in civil or political rights on account of race or color, except as to Indians not taxed, and not be repugnant to the Constitution of the United States and the principles of the Declaration of Independence." Clearly this is an act passed by a Republican-dominated Congress, since focus on the civil and political rights of African Americans points to the still operative differences between the two dominant parties on the questions that fueled the Civil War. In truth, Montana's entrance into statehood has been delayed in large part because of its Democratic-leaning territorial government and delegate—the federal government has not trusted the territory to abide by the values and policies of the winning party in 1865, one that controls the presidency for a full twenty years after the war. The Declaration of Independence will be used to defend proposals before the constitutional convention such as women's suffrage. In a final statement of principle, the Act insists that the new states will demonstrate toleration of diverse religious practices. Balancing the practical with the principled, the legislation assures a federal appropriation of $20,000 to underwrite the costs of Montana's constitutional convention.

The prescriptive document turns increasingly precise about the new state's obligations: to renounce claim to ownership of unappropriated public lands (precisely the issue in play with Marcus Daly and A. B. Hammond's harvesting of timber to feed the copper and silver beast); to pay all outstanding territorial debts; to assure citizens' access to public schools and a land-grant university, in part on land provided by the federal government; to build a penitentiary and a deaf and dumb asylum; and to construct a capitol building to house the freshly minted state government. And so it is that the Enabling Act sets the foundation of principles and dictates the institutions that must house and realize those values. As if to remind the territory of its reward for meeting these conditions, the Act asserts that Montana's senators and representatives will be admitted to Congress. What Congress and President Harrison cannot know is that this final carrot—this evident benefit to Montana—will become the cause of a savage fight between Republicans and Democrats to seat members of the new Congressional delegation, a pathetic replay of the chaos that attended the seating and proceedings of the first territorial legislature at Bannack in December 1864. Federal representatives may be forgiven for wondering whether Montana, for all its passionate pleading for adult status as a state, is ready for the obligations entailed with that transformation.

MARCH

In which Charlie Russell migrates to the Milk River country, B. M. Bower writes a woman's take on the cowboy myth, and James and Pamelia Fergus move to Armells Creek.

Cattle bands are constantly growing smaller in number in Montana and the dashing cow-boy, with spurs, chaps, and revolver, are disappearing. Yet Montana has vast areas of land that will always be worthless for agriculture, though inviting for stock raising and wool growing, so Montana offers advantages in all the varied pursuits without the crowding out or extinction of any. In the growing of cattle, sheep and horses, Montana has only made a beginning.

CHARLIE RUSSELL TURNS TWENTY-FIVE ON MARCH 19, and he's a restless young man. The previous six years he worked as nighthawk for cattle outfits in the Judith Basin, a low-level job that required the hand to watch a quiet herd by night. He spent part of the previous year near the Blood Indians in Canada, an experience that has taken on mythic proportions in Russell lore but was in fact probably more a chance to take a break from labor for a summer in Canada. His knack for art has already been revealed, since "Waiting for a Chinook," the iconic rendering of the disastrous winter of 1886-1887 that signaled the end of the open range on the northern plains, made his name throughout Montana Territory. Yet he writes to a friend in May of 1889, "I have tirde [tried] several times to make a living painting but could not mak it stick and had to go back to

Charles M. Russell and his horse "Monty," 1886. MONTANA HISTORICAL SOCIETY
RESEARCH CENTER PHOTOGRAPH ARCHIVES, HELENA, MONTANA

the range. . . . I expect I will have to ride till the end of my days but I would rather be a poor cow puncher than a poor artist."

In the spring of 1889, he returns to the familiar Judith Basin country to take up night hawking once again, but he finds the place filling with homesteading outfits committed to fencing and haying following the debacle in 1887. So he moves north to the Milk River country, opened up just a year before by the Sweetgrass Treaty that confined the Piegan, Gros Ventres, Assiniboine, and Sioux to three reservations. He will spend the next four years in this country near the Bears Paw Mountains and the towns of Big Sandy and Chinook.

Charlie is looking for that elusive thing he found when he first landed in the territory in 1880, just 16 and determined to discover his true West. Like many a young man from the Midwest, he had been fired by visions of a wide-open life beyond the boredom and routine of a genteel upbringing. He found it for a while, but the open range is fast closing as "trails are plowed under" by new settlers. His storytelling would take on an increasingly rueful cast, for he mourned an evanescent existence that passed before many could know it. Charlie understood the irony of his nostalgia, for it was made possible by the eclipse of native nations, his cowboy life enabled by the confinement of people he deeply admired. His freedom came at the cost of native imprisonment.

His elegiac mood is fed in 1889 by two startling deaths. His cousin Chiles Carr dies in October after being thrown by his horse while working in the Judith Basin. Since he and his cousin had spent much time together and followed similar habits of work and carousing, Charlie finds that premature death sobering in many senses. Even more heartbreaking, Charlie's younger brother Wolfert dies from typhoid in St. Louis that December. Youth is no guarantee of longevity, Charlie discovers, and the good times can pass far too quickly.

Despite his doubts about making a living as an artist, Charlie will pour his longing and remembrance into paintings, sketches, and sculptures, images that feed and challenge the cowboy myth at the same time. A spirit of hilarity, even mockery, often shares room with the iconic images on those canvases, undermining confident assertions of white cultural superiority written into popular novels such as *The Virginian*. Russell's cowboys are frequently playful, if not downright silly, as are his Indians. He reminds his viewer that Montana had been occupied by individuals with mixed motives and compromised dignity, breaking through a shell of often-too-serious reflection on the virtues and vices of the participants in a changing place. He is Theodore Roosevelt's comic doppelgänger.

Russell would also record this edgy sentimentality in his best-selling stories, none better than the original tale, "The Story of the Cowpuncher":

> "Speakin' of cowpunchers," says Rawhide Rawlins, "I'm glad to see in the last few years that them that know the business have been writin' about 'em. It begin to look like they'd be wiped out without a history. Up to a few years ago there's mighty little known about cows and cow people. It was sure amusin' to read some of them old stories about cowpunchin'. You'd think a puncher growed horns an' was haired over.

> ". . . . If they are human, they're a separate species. I'm talkin' about the old-time ones, before the country's strung with wire an' nesters had grabbed all the water, an' a cowpuncher's home was big. It wasn't where he took his hat off, but where he spread his blankets. He ranged from Mexico to the Big Bow River of the north, an' from where the trees get scarce in the east to the old Pacific. He don't need no iron hoss, but covers his country on one that eats

grass an' wears hair. All the tools he needed was saddle, bridle, quirt, hackamore, an' rawhide riatta or seagrass rope; that covered his hoss."

Who better to re-see the West from the woman's perspective than B. M. Bower? Bertha Muzzy arrives in the Big Sandy area in 1889 at the age of eighteen. Her parents have chosen the chanciness of Montana after Sioux Indians moved close to them in Minnesota, the bitter memories of the 1862 battles with the Indians still fresh in upper Midwest memory. Bower will recall a cultured upbringing, even in the apparent deprivation of the Minnesota and Montana hinterlands: "My father taught me music and how to draw plans of houses (he was an architect among other things) and to read 'Paradise Lost' and Dante and H. Rider Haggard and the Bible and the Constitution—and my taste has been extremely catholic since then." Bertha proves a feisty, smart young woman who takes up school teaching as a way to gain some independence from her family. She takes an even more dramatic step toward independence by marrying the older Clayton Bower, a marriage that will produce three children but also a great deal of heartache. Bower will turn to writing as her escape, financially and psychologically, from her abusive husband. Her writing will also become the means to transcribe the myth and realities of cattle country from a woman's perspective.

Bower's daughter Dele will recall her mother sitting at a portable typewriter in their humble cabin, typing away furiously on her fictional works that transport to a world both similar to and quite different from the Montana she experiences on a daily basis. This gifted writer, always considered male by her readers since her initials conceal her gender, gets one of those breaks so vital to a writing life when her family takes up residence on the TL Ranch near the Highwood Mountains. There she meets the

B.(Bertha) M. Bower, Spur Ranch, Texas, [no date] . Montana Historical Society Research Center Photograph Archives, Helena, Montana

real deal, Bertrand Sinclair, a cowboy who knows the cattle business and the cowboy's life like the back of his hand. He becomes her tutor in the ranching life, going so far as to critique her manuscripts for accuracy. While he will become Bower's second husband (another marriage that will end in divorce), Sinclair's major role in her life is that of editor to a dedicated professional writer determined to blend romantic Western storylines with authentic details. Her fiction will aim for that mix of the mythic and the stone-cold sober, offering possibility for happiness but tempering that dream with earned knowledge of how life on the Montana plains can disappoint.

None other than Charlie Russell will play a part in her most enduring fictional success, *Chip of the Flying U*, published in 1904, just two years after *The Virginian*, often called the defining Western fiction. Bower's first novel will feature a cowboy artist no doubt modeled on the playful, gregarious Russell. Through the alchemy of art, Bower will convert her bitter early years in Montana into a bestselling story tapping into the already-powerful cowboy myth. Chip is a skillful cowboy who also possesses a knack for knocking off telling sketches of ranch life. That talent will come clear in a painting titled "The Last Stand," clearly based on an actual painting by CMR. Chip becomes a clever fictional surrogate for Bower herself, since he faces the dilemma of converting artistic talent to paying work, while being forced to conceal his true identity (his breakthrough painting is at first attributed to the ranch owner's sister, affectionately called "Little Doc" since she is a licensed physician).

Coming closer to Bower's lived experience as Montanan and writer, *Lonesome Land*, a novel published in 1912 and now considered her best fiction, provides a semi-autobiographical portrait of the woman writer. The novel draws strength from its focus on a complex female protagonist, Valerie Peyson, who arrives in her new home of Hope, Montana, to marry a cowboy.

The opening landscape description sets both scene and tone for the action to follow:

> In northern Montana there lies a great, lonely stretch of prairie land, gashed deep where flows the Missouri. Indeed, there are many such—big, impassive, impressive in their very loneliness, in summer given over to the winds and the meadow larks and to the shadows fleeing always over the hilltops. Wild range cattle feed there and grow sleek and fat for the fall shipping of beef. At night the coyotes yap quaveringly and prowl abroad after the long-eared jack rabbits, which bounce away at their hunger-driven approach. In winter it is not good to be there; even the beasts shrink then from the bleak, level reaches, and shun the still bleaker heights.

Talk about a fall from innocence to experience! The cultured, refined, prim eastern woman has just arrived in her new home, a place she has never seen, prepared to marry the cowboy of her dreams and to live in a kind of pastoral bliss. The novel sets about disabusing Val of each and every one of these illusions nurtured by popular images of the West. Her cowboy husband will prove more dedicated to drink than romance, and the land will demand far more of her physically and psychologically than she could anticipate.

In a sense, Bower may have been staging a contest between her first and second husbands through this fictional narrative. Manley Fleetwood, Val's ne'er-do-well husband, seems to embody many of the less appealing traits of Clayton Bower, while Kent Burnett, the cowboy who saves Val from a devastating prairie fire and becomes Val's pal, including serving as critic for her writing as she begins her professional career, seems an idealized stand-in for Sinclair. Bower exploits familiar conventions from the Western made famous by the likes of Wister, Zane Grey, and Bower herself. Fleetwood, after all, turns to rustling to make up for losses from that terrible fire and so takes on qualities of the antagonist in Westerns. Burnett, on the other hand, shares many qualities with the Virginian, appearing smart, playful, respectful, and tough, all at the same time.

Yet the novel has a deeper game to play than simply recirculating stereotypes from popular Westerns. The daunting landscape revealed in the novel's opening paragraph transforms Val: "Of a truth, [Val] was different. . . . She was not the prim, perfectly well-bred young woman he had met at the train. Lonesome Land was doing its work. She was beginning to think as an individual—as a woman; not merely as a member of conventional society." Bower may be poking fun at her own younger self, one who carried snobbish assumptions about Montana when she arrived from Minnesota, one who fled to a bad marriage to get out from under her parents, one who needed to adopt writing as a trade to support herself and her children when her first marriage went smash. The transparent symbolism of the fire burning Val's illusions to the ground early in the novel—linked to Kent's last name of "Burnett"—reveals a clever established novelist working at the top of her game. She burns out any lingering prospect for a meaningful marriage to the alcoholic Manley, clearing the ground for new growth with Kent.

Nannie Alderson will famously write, "There was an old and rather brutal saying out west, to the effect that this was a great country for men and horses, but hell on women and cattle." Bower amends that statement by showing the West could indeed be hard on an ill-prepared, selfish, weak male (Manley) and more promising for a determined, adaptive, talented woman (Val). After Manley meets his untimely death, breaking forever the frayed bond to Val, she chooses to return east to weigh her options. Kent's relationship with her remains one of companion and avowed suitor, rather than consummated lover or husband, and the reader can only infer he may join Val to formalize their relationship. The novel's energies lead toward Val's maturation and independence, not some predetermined return to the marriage bond. Bower's West is hardly the one of familiar movies, television shows, and novels. Val is a complex character who survives a desperately bad marriage to plot her future for herself.

JAMES FERGUS, EARLY MONTANA EMIGRANT, SHARES HIS BY turns waspish and affectionate description of the reigning town of the county named for him on the 25th day of spring's first month:

> The writer has just made a visit to Lewistown, the county seat of Fergus County. As many of your readers know, it is situated on Big Spring creek, a beautiful, clear mill stream, having its source in springs in the foot of the Snowies, in the southeast corner of Judith Basin. It has two excellent hotels, two good general merchandise stores and a bank. . . .

> It contains two blacksmith shops, two butcher shops and two saddler shops, two livery and feed stables, two churches, a school with 75 pupils, a sawmill, and, unfortunately, four lawyers, three doctors and too many saloons. . . .

> For a Republican county, it has a good set of officers. Frank Wright the efficient treasurer is unfortunately confined to his room with boils where Job had them. Frank Smith, the good looking young county attorney, is said to be an aspirant for member of the constitutional convention, for matrimony and every other good thing that comes his way. Meagher, the probate judge, is a bashful looking young man, but is said to be a good authority on all subjects where ladies are not interested.

Pamelia and James Fergus. MONTANA HISTORICAL SOCIETY RESEARCH
CENTER PHOTOGRAPH ARCHIVES, HELENA, MONTANA

> Like most of our unorganized frontier towns, Lewistown
> is careless about keeping its streets clear—free from
> sweepings, trash, mud holes, and her stable yards and
> back lots free from piles of stinking manure. With these
> exceptions it is a pretty pleasant place, and has a good
> friendly sociable population.

The passage captures the man in all his fussiness, shrewd-
ness, and candor. Seventy-five years old at the time of this writing, Fergus has become a living legend in the territory about
to become a state. He landed in Bannack in 1862, wrote to his
wife, Pamelia, and his children to join him in Virginia City in
1864, migrated to the Helena region, then made a risky move
to his final homestead on Armells Creek in 1880. The creek was
named for Augustin Hamell or Armell, a Métis who established
a trading post on this very creek in the mid-1840s. James and
his partner/son Andrew drove 900 cattle and 100 horses 200
miles to their new ranch land. The move had been risky because
members of the Assiniboine, Piegan, Gros Ventre, and Lakota
nations would frequently hunt and camp nearby, increasingly
stressed for food as the bison were systematically removed from
this glorious land and annuities consistently failed to material-
ize. The Métis also hunted this region, for in 1880 Granville Stuart witnessed fifty families searching for buffalo in one of the few
remaining areas where the life source still flourished. In fact, the
Métis started the settlement that has come to be known as Lewistown, though Fergus does not include them in his newspaper
account.

Fergus's migration to this seemingly open land is so typical
of his restless longing for the next best place. Perhaps it's his immigrant nature, a son of Scotland transplanted to America in the
1830s, failed founder of the Minnesota town of Little Falls, and
searcher for gold and opportunity in Colorado and Montana in
the 1860s. A member of James Fisk's first Northern Overland

Expedition in 1862, Fergus arrived early in a place being defined as "Montana." Notably hard-working, conscientious, and opinionated, he would be selected for public office often, including his role as caretaker of the poor in Virginia City when eight-year-old Calamity Jane knocked on his door on a cold December night in 1864. Stoutly Republican in a strongly Democratic territory, despite the acerbic tone of his mention of Republican officers in Lewistown, Fergus is deeply disappointed when he is not elected as delegate to the Constitutional Convention convening in Helena in just three months. Given his political leanings, his diehard friendship with Wilbur Sanders, lawyer for Huie Pock and other Chinese in their lawsuit against organizers of a Chinese boycott in Butte, this does not surprise. Yet Fergus's frugal nature will cause him to question the political leadership of public officers of both parties, for he is ever on the search for misuse and over expenditure of his hard-earned money. Though goldmining anchored him in Montana in the 1860s, Fergus had long since converted to a ranching life, which explains his aggressive pursuit of a law favorable to the territory rather than the mining industries so dominant in Butte and elsewhere: Tax the total assessed value of the mining properties rather than the net profits from said mines. Though he would not be able to make this case to the Constitutional Convention, his hyperactive pen will not be silenced, and he will make his plea for ranching interests until his dying days.

As he writes this description of Fergus County's seat, he is still mourning the passing of Pamelia in 1887. While apparently not given to frequent displays of affection, the couple had found a steady, effective partnership, one that would survive James's quest for space and status. James shared this memorable portrait of their enduring marriage:

> Our Children being all married but Andrew he seldom at home and me an invilid [sic] we were always together and

thought far more of each other than we did when we were young. I think people of good sense generally do, having lived so long together they become so used to each others ways become more like each other are more forgiving and one becomes as it were a necessity to the other, I know it was so with us.

Though Pamelia was initially alarmed by the move to the Judith country, compelled to leave behind the comforts of Helena, she seems to have adapted to this last homestead: "Madame fails [struggles physically] less than I do, works hard, doing nearly all the work for nine men, makes butter, raises chickens, has flowers and plants indoors and out and is always busy." Yet Pamelia could suffer bouts of intense loneliness, especially the first year at Armells Creek when even their nearest neighbor, Granville Stuart, some twenty miles distant, had not yet brought his family to the cattle range.

Wilbur Sanders delivered the eulogy at her funeral, acknowledging Pamelia's hard work, devotion to family, and agnosticism:

Friends—the dead wife, mother and friend who lies here belonged to no religious sect, believed in no religious dogma and desired no religious services over her remains. The wishes of the living will be kept as a sacred contract with the dead. While she could not understand how she could live after death, or locate a heaven or a hell, she clearly comprehended the duties appertaining to her station in life and in their performances was an obedient child, a faithful wife, a loving mother, a true friend and an honest woman, performing her full duty in all stations in life, beloved by all, and leaving not an enemy behind. When our end comes may as much be said of us.

APRIL

In which Theodore Roosevelt narrates the triumph of American civilization, John Stands in Timber describes a Cheyenne attempt at plowing, and Andrew Garcia mourns the end of his Indian days.

_____

Seven car loads of passengers have arrived recently at Glasgow, a station on the St. Paul & Manitoba railroad, 370 miles east of Helena, and to which place the railroad shops now at Minot are to be removed.

_____

The beginning of the American republic now stands forth an era far more important than that for Magna Charta or the Petition of Rights. Its centennial will, therefore, be celebrated in New York city with all the enthusiasm of the first inauguration added to the confidence born of a hundred years' success.

_____

ON THE FIRST DAY OF THE FOURTH MONTH THEODORE Roosevelt finishes writing volume two of *Winning of the West*, a series justifying Anglo-American conquest of the North American landmass. It's as though Theodore were responding with his usual bravado to the protests of Young Man Afraid of His Horses, Louis Riel, and other advocates for indigenous rights. In Roosevelt's mind, he has earned the right to make this case, not only because he is a wealthy social and political leader from New York City, but also because he has built a ranch in the badlands of Dakota Territory, the Elkhorn, located in the very country crossed by General Alfred Sully's troops on

Theodore Roosevelt, posing in his hunting clothing, 1885. THEODORE ROOSEVELT CENTER

their forced march through the badlands during the summer of 1864 following the Battle of Killdeer Mountain. He named his ranch for locked elk horns found near his temporary western home, indicating a mighty struggle between two bull elks, a fitting symbol for Roosevelt's view of western settlement.

Bereft, heart-broken, and depleted of energy following the death of his beloved young wife, Alice, Roosevelt retreated to the western plains in 1884 to restore himself, to find vigor, to become truly a man again—his wife's death had unmanned him. Though somewhat comic in his buckskin garb, he proved a hearty, enthusiastic part-time inhabitant of the plains, shooting game, running cattle, punching out an occasional bully, and capturing a thief or two. He will receive high praise from one of the most credible cowboys of the era, Teddy Blue Abbott: "Rich men's sons from the East were nothing new as far as I was concerned. The range in the eighties was as full of them as a dog's hair of fleas, and some of them were good fellows and some were damn fools. Quite a few, like Teddy Roosevelt . . . made good hands and everybody liked them." Roosevelt also participated in stop-and-go fashion in the Montana Stockgrowers Association, writing with obvious relish, "A true 'cow town' is worth seeing,—such a one as Miles City, for instance, especially at the time of the annual meeting of the great Montana Stock-raisers' Association. Then the whole place is full to overflowing, the importance of the meeting and the fun of the attendant frolics, especially the horse-races, drawing from the surrounding ranch country many hundreds of men of every degree. . . ." TR was so all in with the Stockgrowers that he volunteered to join Stuart's Stranglers in their roundup of alleged rustlers in 1884. Granville Stuart politely declined the offer, hinting that the vigilantes would prefer to remain more secretive than Teddy's presence might allow.

Roosevelt represents with unusual clarity the confident belief in the American mission to colonize and tame the West. Unapologetic, surprisingly un-self-reflective for such an intelligent

Main Street, Miles City, 1888. MONTANA HISTORICAL SOCIETY RESEARCH CENTER PHOTOGRAPH ARCHIVES, HELENA, MONTANA

man, Roosevelt embraces the racialist belief that Anglo-American culture fulfilled its world-historical destiny by conquering "savages" and installing American institutions in the West. His sanguine views on extermination of the great bison herds are typical:

> While the slaughter of the buffalo has been in places needless and brutal, and while it is to be greatly regretted that the species is likely to become extinct. . . it must be remembered that its continued existence in any numbers was absolutely incompatible with any thing but a very sparse settlement of the country; and that its destruction was the condition precedent upon the advance of white civilization in the West. . . . Above all, the extermination of the buffalo was the only way of solving the Indian question. As long as this large animal of the chase existed, the Indians simply could not be kept on reservations, and always had an ample supply of meat on hand to support them in the event of a war; and its disappearance was the only method of forcing them to at least partially abandon their savage mode of life. From the standpoint of humanity at large, the extermination of the buffalo has been a blessing.

In one sense TR's values are as old as Western European culture, reaffirming belief in a "Passage to India" that would transport a set of values across the Atlantic Ocean, across the American continent, across the Pacific Ocean, across Asia, closing the circle of domination in Europe. In another sense, those values are as new as the United States, with its manifest ambition to control as much of a continent as possible, and to explain that reach as fulfillment of a distinctive purpose called "an empire of liberty" by none other than Thomas Jefferson.

Roosevelt's bona fides as a progressive reformer and conservation advocate only complicate our understanding of his imperialist cocksureness. But these seemingly contradictory parts make a seamless whole: world history dictated that United States' civilization would be extended through space and time, but that civilization's leaders must assure the mission remains pure, that civilization ethical, and wilderness provides the literal and figurative ground for "Nature's Nation." If nothing else, untamed lands offer the tonic for a potentially debased elite class, the means to prove one's mettle, to harden one's hands and soul, to become fit for the strenuous life of world leader. TR has done his work in the West, providing the most stout, unapologetic defense of American conquest.

Roosevelt would spend less and less time at his beloved Elkhorn Ranch, realizing that his second marriage and an accelerating political career would not allow him time to retreat to the Dakota badlands for recuperation and restoration. He also recognized his Dakota retreat had been forever changed by immigrants such as himself. Not only bison but deer, elk, and bear had been all but exterminated from the region. The winter of 1886-1887 that figured so prominently in Montana's story also devastated western Dakota, leading to the near-collapse of Medora, the community that anchored TR's ranching life. In just a few years, an area that supported indigenous people for hundreds of years was depleted and debased. In TR's mordant words, "The best days of ranching are over. . . ." Roosevelt wrote books such as *Ranch Life and Hunting Trails*, published in 1888, to capture the evanescent West. He actively promotes the cowboy myth so resonant, so alluring down to the present time.

Roosevelt also shares much of the affection and anxiety for the frontier as Frederick Jackson Turner, whose talk "The Significance of the Frontier in American History," which will be delivered in 1893 during the American celebration of Columbus's discovery of the New World, will shape American understanding of the West for a century. The 1890 census asserted that the American frontier had ended. Turner will take that declaration as a sign of irrevocable change to the American character. The frontier defined, created, assured a unique culture in the United States by compelling settlers to adapt, improvise, discover democracy in unstable transition zones, the space where "civilization" meets "wilderness." In Turner's words, "The peculiarity of American institutions is, the fact that they have been compelled to adapt themselves to the changes of an expanding people—to the changes involved in crossing a continent, in winning a wilderness, and in developing at each area of this progress out of the primitive economic and political conditions of the frontier into the complexity of city life."

Turner not only will praise the frontier as formative experience but fret about the consequences of losing that incubator of American character. In many ways Roosevelt's nostalgia and Turner's thesis capture a peculiar mixture of pride, memory, and dread when Americans cast their minds westward "across the wide Missouri." Something goes slack, relaxed, even playful when remembering the already-missing "West," yet knowledge of the frontier era's closing—truly a fall from innocence to experience—raises questions about the sustainability, virtue, and sheer pleasure of life in more settled regions, where bureaucracy, industry, railroads, and capital reign. Myths such as the frontier thesis cause Americans to forget as much as remember. Caught up in the dream of the cowboy paradise that vanished so quickly on the western plains in the 1880s, they can forget the violence, cruelty, and pain of seizing control of Indian homelands. Nostalgia washes away guilt and shame.

This complex of emotions helps explain Roosevelt's role—along with George Bird Grinnell's—in designing the Boone and Crockett exhibit for the Columbian Exposition in Chicago. As the designers explain to members, "The club erected a long, low cabin of unhewn logs. . . of the kind in which the first hunters and frontier settlers dwelt. . . . Elk and deer hides were scattered over the floor or tacked to the walls." A "white-capped prairie schooner" stood in front of the cabin. With evident pride, Roosevelt and Grinnell could claim their exhibit showed "a typical and peculiar phase of American national development . . . life on the frontier."

A NORTHERN CHEYENNE WITNESS, JOHN STANDS IN TIMBER, recalls efforts to teach his people to plow:

> The early days of the reservation was when the white men or farmers were teaching the Indians how to farm, how to plant seeds and all those things. The very first thing they had to know was how to plow; how to hold the walking plow some days. One day they gathered at the agency, and it was announced to the Indians all the men must fix themselves up and they were going to teach them how to plow the ground.
>
> In those days . . . there were a few that could interpret but not very good. The day came they were supposed to gather. A lot of them came, and a lot of women came too to see how they were going to farm. A farmer was there and he had a team and a plow ready to go. After they all got there they sat in a row to watch the white man plow the ground. So he started out plowing, go around maybe once or twice. He must have had a list of the names, because he called out the first one that was supposed to try to plow. So he got up and walked toward the plow. They had misunderstood. They thought they were supposed to put on a good costume, so they had feathers on their heads, and necklaces and beaded moccasins and fancy leggings. . . .
>
> They all had fancy Indian clothing. What the foreman meant was to put on pants and shoes and gloves, but they

did not understand it; they thought they had to put on their best costumes.

Montana's most voluble storyteller didn't like to talk about 1889. When interviewed for the Montana Writers Project in 1940, a classic Work Progress Administration program, Andrew Garcia will refuse to say much about his first ranch in the Clark Fork Valley west of Missoula, where he moved in 1887 with his second Pend d'Oreille wife, Mal-lit-lay-tay. He will tell the recorder that he arrived near Fish Creek by way of Flathead Lake and Missoula, after living for a time with the Pend d'Oreille nation in Idaho. Other records hint at the cause for Garcia's reticence about this phase of his life: Mal-lit-lay-tay dies in 1889, cutting Garcia's final ties with his extraordinary youth among the Indians and military men of the 1870s.

Garcia now, finally, gives up his life in-between native and American worlds. It will be ten more years before he remarries, and this time it's a white woman, Barbara Voll. He claims a second ranch at Fish Creek, the home he will occupy for the remaining 44 years of his life. He will spend those years in the often frustrating effort to get his story on paper, becoming a memorable member of the Society of Montana Pioneers, corresponding with Lucullus McWhorter, a man dedicated to defending Nez Perce rights, and writing compulsively at night, after a hard day's work, the manuscripts that will ultimately become *Tough Trip through Paradise*. In the poignant words of the memoir that will be made out of his rough-cut manuscripts, "All of my associates of those rough and ready years have crossed the Great Divide, and the Squaw Kid wanderer awaits the final journey."

For a time, what a world he had seen, what a life he had lived. Born in the Rio Grande country of Texas in 1855, he witnessed the intense conflicts over control of the land among Americans, Mexicans, and Comanches. He would carry those memories—

Andrew Garcia. MONTANA HISTORICAL SOCIETY RESEARCH CENTER PHOTOGRAPH
ARCHIVES, HELENA, MONTANA

that bitter understanding—north with him when he first came to Montana Territory in 1868 with his uncle, a wrangler for the U. S. Army. Garcia threw in his lot with the territory in 1876, returning as a wrangler for the military on his own. And so it was that he served in Nelson Miles' campaign against the Nez Perce during the infamous travail of 1877. The memory of the final encounter in the Bears Paw Mountains will haunt Garcia and take on even darker shades of tragedy as his story unfolds. In 1878, he decided to set up a "trading emporium" in the Musselshell River country with the ne'er-do-well trapper "Beaver Tom," an alcoholic partner who showed far more acumen at stealing Garcia's money and goods than at helping him sell supplies to the wandering indigenous peoples in this confused, disorienting time following the Battle of the Little Bighorn and the Nez Perce flight. The only profit Garcia drew from this dubious enterprise was many good stories about his negligent partner, the Indian peoples who visit their camp, and his soon-to-be wife, In-Who-Lise, a woman of the Nez Perce nation.

That In-Who-Lise possessed Garcia will become clear in his choosing to title his manuscript for her. She will inspire what is unquestionably the emotional highlight of *Tough Trip*, their return to the Big Hole Battlefield, where her sister and father died and she was seriously wounded. Garcia's prose will take on dark Gothic overtones as he describes wandering among the remains of a brutal assault on the fleeing Nez Perce in the summer of 1877. In-Who-Lise discovered her father's corpse had been dragged from its temporary burial spot and scalped, only intensifying her mourning: Her father had not been granted a peaceful afterlife. Given Garcia's role in capturing her people before they could cross the Canadian border, his Catholic guilt compounded the pain of this fraught journey to the site of an American atrocity.

Garcia will share with McWhorter his primary reasons for telling his life's story: To provide an alternative version of the history of Indian-white conflict, which he believes is written to help the white conquerors cover their sins. Garcia by no means absolves Indian peoples of their own forms of cruelty, for he has witnessed occasions of their gratuitous violence. Instead, he is offended by the tendency to whitewash American conquest with Western romantic fables and military glory. He also feels compelled to defend the character of Indian women, whom he sees as demeaned by stereotypes as lecherous, romanticized, or downtrodden. His account of his travels with In-Who-Lise provides a complex sense of her desires and ambitions, undermining just such stereotypes. With his usual humor, Garcia shows how the married couple can at times think and act at cross purposes, while remaining very much a couple. So it is that Garcia communicates deep mourning upon In-Who-Lise's death at the hands of the Blackfeet in the Marias Mountains. Following that loss he marries two Pend' Oreille women, Squis-squis and Mat-il-lay-tay. He attests to their decency and their excellence as wives. No wonder his third wife's death depletes him of any desire to return to that moment of loss in 1889, the turning point in his life, as he will never again live among the Indian peoples he presents with such complexity, humor, and affection. In the words of Ben Stein, the man who created *Tough Trip* out of Gracia's jumbled manuscripts, "He knew that after leaving the Indians he was never again so happy. This was the force behind his urge to write. As a homesteader and civilized white man, he felt like a leopard in a cage. Few white men had seen what he had, and none of them were writers."

Following Garcia's death and the successful publication of *Tough Trip*, many will doubt the veracity of his seeming tall tale. How to account for this wild story of scoundrels and saints in the wilds of Montana Territory? The prose itself, a wildly inventive medley of voices, seems to undercut the tale's credibility. Yet letters unquestionably written in Garcia's hand echo that odd mix of formal and informal language. And Garcia's commitment to faithful recording of his past, on display in his many letters to McWhorter, points to a memoirist faithful to his past but willing to stretch the truth a bit. After all, Garcia came of age in central Montana at a time when storytelling around campfires was a way of life and men proved their mettle by entertaining their comrades. Charlie Russell arrived only a few years after Garcia.

Given the Squaw Kid's evident compulsion to publish his story, what prevented him from bringing his tale to print? Garcia will share with McWhorter his fourth wife's disdain for the project, her disapproval dampening his spirits and compelling him to write at night after his day's chores are done. For all his extravagant experiences and phrase-making, this may be Garcia's most impressive gift to future Montanans: his unstinting effort to tell a much more complex story of native/white life in the Treasure State than often allowed by official narratives and mass media. Even if the book that finally emerges from his disjointed manuscripts will court doubt and derision, Garcia captures a contemporary reader's attention and provokes hard questions about how diverse peoples treated each other on the contested ground of Montana in that difficult time of transition.

MAY

In which Mary Gleim begins building her Missoula empire, Spokane becomes Montana's most famous racehorse, and ranchers petition to remove the Northern Cheyenne.

Eph. Harrison and Ccl. Scheetz will shortly start out on a surveying tour. They are going to establish the eastern and southern boundaries of the Crow reservation. . . . When this work is completed they will start in the surveying of four townships near Ekaleka.

Responsible parties just in from Samedor report a large party of Pine Ridge Indians, led by Grasshopper, have come into the Tongue River agency for the purpose of getting up a sun dance among the Cheyennes. The Cheyennes are in sympathy with the Sioux and the sun dance will certainly be held unless the Cheyennes are overawed by the presence of a large body of troops. The Crow outbreak of last summer had its origin in a sun dance gotten up by Grasshopper and held at the same place.

SHE MOVES WITH FIERCE FORCE, LARGE AND UNSTOPPAble, gaudy, garish, and determined, Mary Gleeson Gleim, reigning madam of Missoula's underworld, a dealer in opiates, diamonds, Chinese laborers, and women of the night. She buys her first building on Front Strcct in May of 1889, having arrived the year before from St. Louis with her husband. Apparently Mary had seduced this not-very-bright spouse with her not-always-evident charms. She may simply have possessed more competence in building and managing wealth than he. That first purchase will lead to ownership of eight separate buildings, each reputed to be a den of sin though operating under the cover of more respectable businesses (boarding houses for women, furniture stores, and more).

Prostitution is an important, even sanctioned business in 1889. Respectable society condemns the practice in public while acceding to it in private. Prostitution is the second largest business for women in Helena during the 1880s. In towns dominated by single men, soiled doves provide a safety valve for male desire. Prominent early Montana capitalists such as Anton Holter invest in Butte brothels, while madams become notable businesswomen. Besides, the prostitutes themselves prove beneficial to local economies, for they must acquire fine clothing, jewelry, and other accessories to ply their trade. As Rose Gordon observes of the "Tenderloin District" of White Sulphur Springs in the 1880s and 90s: "These women were great spenders and the Merchants missed their trade[;] while they were not a moral asset they were a commercial asset. . . ."

Yet even granting the tacit acceptance of prostitution, Mary Gleim must have tested the limits of community tolerance for her trade. An Irish immigrant who will carry as large a reputation as her 200-pound frame, she will prove a godsend for lawyers, since she initiates and inspires so many lawsuits through her fits of rage. She never sees a fight she doesn't want to pick. She is at war with the world, the source of that rage never fully revealed. Perhaps she was born angry, or perhaps she was made that way by the cruelty and slights immigrant women must endure.

Given her cantankerous nature and mysterious business dealings, "Mother Gleim," a nickname spoken with sarcasm, respect, and fear, makes for excellent newspaper copy, especially in a time when journalists do not hesitate to produce highly colored prose. When her violent outbursts culminate with conviction for attempted murder, the *Anaconda Standard* will report her sentencing with ill-concealed delight:

> Mary Gleim, who was convicted of attempting to kill Bobby Burns by placing dynamite under his dwelling house, was at 4 o'clock this afternoon [September 14, 1894], sentenced by Judge Woody to 14 years in the penitentiary at Deer Lodge and to pay the costs of the prosecution. . . . This is the maximum penalty and the judge wasted but little time in giving it to her. . . . It was expected that she would make a scene in the court room, but she took the sentence coolly and bridled her hitherto ungovernable tongue. She will be taken to Deer Lodge Sunday morning. This rids the city of one of its most dangerous characters.

Gleim will win a temporary reprieve from her incarceration when it turns out one of the jurors who convicted her was not in fact an American citizen. However, she will not use this freedom to her best advantage, for as another newspaper story recounts, "Mother Gleim broke loose this afternoon for the first time since her release from the pen at Deer Lodge and, as a result of her operations, Billy Preneveau, John Gleim's man Friday, is a total wreck. Billy claims that Mrs. Gleim punched him in the cheek, knocking him down, and then beat him over the arms and legs with the leg from a table. . . . Mrs. Gleim will probably be tried tomorrow."

Gleim's obituary in her hometown newspaper on February 23, 1914, will provide a fitting climax to these sensationalized stories:

> Mary Gleim is dead. Her militant spirit passed from its mortal frame late yesterday afternoon. . . . Mrs. Gleim

was about 65 years old and had been a resident of Missoula since 1888. She was a woman of mystery. Ever since she came to Missoula she had been a picturesque figure. There are few persons in this city who had not heard of her . . .

Perhaps there are some persons who know the history of this strange woman's life, but it is not likely that it will ever be told. She was a woman of contraries. In her prime, she possessed remarkable physical strength. Intellectually, she was wonderfully endowed. She was educated and possessed many qualities of refinement. But she was of the underworld; from the time of her arrival in Missoula until her death, she associated herself with the element against whom the bars of society are set. She owned much property in the restricted [red light] district and this was one of the sources of her revnue [sic]. . . .

While in the state prison, Mrs. Gleim was attacked in the yard one day by a woman who had been sent to the pen from Missoula, and was badly beaten. She was never as vigorous after she came back from prison.

With all her faults, Mrs. Gleim had a generous heart. There are many acts of kindness credited to her. But she was a relentless hater and during the days when she figured so prominently in the battles of a wide-open town, she fought some hard battles. These were real battles, too. She fought physically and was able to handle any man who ever went against her, even when he was clothed in official authority.

Mother Gleim arrives and thrives at a moment in the late 1880s and early 90s when Missoula is indeed a "wide-open town," full of young men on the make, drawn by railroads, timber, and mining. Fittingly, Gleim's tombstone will be placed so it faces the railroad, allowing her to wave to her best customers as they ride by. She demonstrates that despite efforts to control the opium trade, that business remains alive and well as an undercurrent of the Montana economy. She also shows that a strong woman can take on men physically, intellectually, and legally, though most would not choose to emulate her life.

In a world of horses, one horse stands tall: Spokane. A David who slays Goliath at the biggest race of all, the Kentucky Derby, on May 9. Who could have foretold a Montana horse's victory over the imperious Proctor Knott, a Kentucky-foaled horse reputed to be an exceptional three-year-old? Yet a distracted favored horse and a determined Montana thoroughbred will defeat the odds. The horse lives up to the meaning of his name in the Spokane language: "Children of the Sun."

Foaled in the famous Doncaster Barn near Twin Bridges in the beautiful Ruby River country, the Tobacco Root Mountains towering to the east, Spokane stands in for all those horses Montana breeds and raises. Montanans live by and through horses, the primary means for travel, transportation, and work, and important companions, too, in the wide-open country that can breed loneliness as well as foals. Informal horse racing is a common diversion for Montanans lacking other forms of entertainment. Stuart's Stranglers had gone after assumed horse thieves, not cattle rustlers. Thoroughbreds, the royalty of horses, become symbols of a region's superiority in raising the finest specimens of these essential animals. So much more is at stake at that Kentucky Derby in 1889 than winning a prestigious race.

Spokane is a chestnut colt that has caught the eye of the racing public. But does he possess the fighting spirit and the nerve to triumph on this big stage? The horses break clean at the start, with Proctor Knott claiming a lead over Spokane until the back-

Portrait of Spokane, the Montana horse that won the 1889 Kentucky Derby.

stretch. And then the Kentucky horse does something odd, un-expected, perhaps a result of nerves or pent-up energy: He veers to the right, breaking his momentum, and Spokane takes the lead by following a straight route on the rail. The race is not over, however, for Proctor Knott shows impressive closing speed, coming up fast as the finish line approaches. Wait, who won in that split second across the line? The officials declare Spokane the winner by, as one reporter puts it, "a flaming nostril." And he wins in record time, the fastest recorded at the one-and-one-half-mile length for a race now run at one-and-one-quarter-mile. Some question the result, claiming the Knott edged ahead by the end, but Spokane's victory holds. He will back it up with a triumph at another race on the famed track, the Clark Stakes, and even more impressively, at the American Derby in Chicago in June, paying the winner $17,000, a princely sum.

While understandably proud of the only winner of the Ken-tucky Derby from Montana, citizens tended to exaggerate the odds and the wonder of the achievement. How thrilling to imag-ine a raw horse, the living symbol of the wild West, besting the overly refined elite horses from "back East." The legend takes on an especially colorful cast when a reporter for a St. Paul news-paper imagines Spokane's special diet, drawn from Montana's untamed landscape: "the raw-boned brute sniffed the rare air of the Rockies, and was fed the wildflower of the Indians. He grew big and lusty, his sides expanded, his limbs became rock-strong, and turning into his third year the Illinois outcast was a thing of equine beauty." In truth, Armstrong the owner struck it rich in mining and so is able to invest impressive sums in Spokane's care, feeding, and training. Spokane was sired by J. B. Haggin's Hyder Ali, the product of elite horse stock, and trained as a two-year-old at a top-tier farm in Tennessee. Perceptive observers consider Spokane a legitimate threat to take the Derby, and the betting does not overwhelmingly favor Proctor Knott. And con-trary to the myth, Proctor Knott will go on to defeat Spokane in three subsequent races—Montana's most renowned horse will never regain that winning form.

Petition to the President
He is solicited to take a hand in the Cheyenne Reserve matter.
A Petition and Complaint which Embodies Great Points
Upon which it is Founded.

The Cheyennes Must Go.
A United Movement by Custer County for the Extinction
of the Cheyenne Reservation.

So screams a page-one headline in the May 28 issue of the *Daily Yellowstone Journal*. The paper clearly favors the petitioners' cause, for the article that follows urges readers to study the document closely before affixing their signatures. To their credit, the complainants are admirably clear in stating their demands:

> The Undersigned citizens of Custer county, irrespective of party, do most earnestly pray that you may cause that portion of our county known as "The Northern Cheyenne Indian reservation," located on Tongue River, Lame Deer and Rosebud creeks, to be thrown open and restored to the public domain . . . .

> This reservation was created by an executive order after white settlers had taken up homes within its limits, and the order preserves to these settlers the rights of occupancy and ownership, but it also surrounds each of them with Indian territory, over which the Indians can and do roam at will, committing continual trespass on the cattle, sheep and crops of the white settlers, who have no redress and can have no escape save by deserting the homes on

which they have spent years of toil, to renew the struggle elsewhere.

The petitioners justify this demand by asserting the reservation blocks them from trailing their cattle to the railhead at Miles City, making their ranching operations unprofitable and depleting the county seat of tax revenues. They further claim the Cheyenne are not practicing agriculture as assumed when the reservation was created and have in fact "steadily retrograded in the past five or six years." The advocates conclude by recommending the Northern Cheyenne occupy part of the nearby Crow Reservation, freeing the Tongue and Rosebud drainages for white settlement. In an attempt to seal the case for removal, the newspaper editor adds a gratuitous swipe at advocates for Indian rights in Washington D.C., assuring President Harrison that "Indian department inspectors . . . have reported that the Indians ought to be removed," but "that pigheaded and ignorant coterie of philanthropists yclept the 'Indian Defense Committee,' who knowing less of the Indian character than they do of the Kingdom of Heaven, falsely assume that every movement of this kind is a deeply laid scheme to rob the savage."

Contrast this urgent, patronizing plea with the words of Little Wolf, explaining to an agent in Indian Territory (later Oklahoma) in 1878 why his people needed to return to the Tongue River country after their exile for participating in the Battle of the Little Bighorn:

> We have come to ask the agent that we be sent home
> to our own country in the mountains. My people were
> raised there, in a land of pines and clear, cold rivers.
> There, we were always healthy for there was meat enough
> for all. . . . this is not a good place for us. . . . Before another year has passed, we may all be dead, and there will
> be none of us left to travel north.

Two nations, each desiring this land south of Miles City, but seeing it through entirely different lenses. Both claim the place as home, yet how different their motives, their beliefs, their methods. The white settlers read the region through economics and individual well-being, interpreting the beautiful if tough land as a resource for extracting wealth. The Northern Cheyenne see the land as a common place, a shared holding, a nurturing mother, a sheltering father.

But how did the Northern Cheyenne come to be on this reservation in the first place, given Little Wolf's poignant plea fully 1,500 miles south of their homeland? Homesick, hungry, and displaced, the Cheyenne, under Dull Knife and Little Wolf, fled Indian Territory for the unknown. While they sought home, they knew they might be stepping into death. Yet as they repeatedly told their captors, they would rather die than remain in a strange land, humid and bereft of game, far from the dry air and clear vision of the Tongue River country. The journey was bitter, frightening, exhilarating, hopeless, and hopeful all at once. The leaders insisted their people strike at soldiers only, never civilians, and on the whole their order seems to have been fulfilled. Yet fight they must, in hit or miss fashion, so typical of warfare on the plains, when a people could disappear into a river valley or under a swale of land or in the shadow of sandstone bluffs. Viewed from a distance, the plains might seem flat, open, accessible, yet traveling through them one is reminded time and again that she is traveling across the bottom of a very old, long-gone ocean, for the land undulates, buckles, rises and falls, swells and recedes.

Little Wolf and Dull Knife succeeded in evading capture all the way from Indian Territory to the Platte River. They found game to sustain their people, even as they fought several engagements with troops who seemed to come out of nowhere. As if by magic they would appear and disappear on those mysterious plains. Crossing those legendary rivers, the Arkansas and Re-

Little Wolf and Dull Knife, 1873. PHOTOGRAPH BY WILLIAM HENRY JACKSON. CHIEF DULL KNIFE COLLEGE

publican, the Cheyenne protected the women and children and mainly avoided towns and ranches. But at the Platte the leaders determined to go their separate ways, perhaps to complicate the soldiers' attempts to find and punish them. Ultimately, Little Wolf continued on a northern line, relishing the prospect of his homeland. For a time, his people went undetected, but their luck would not hold, for scouts from Fort Keogh on the Yellowstone discovered their whereabouts. The military leaders, impressed and even moved by the Cheyenne perseverance in the face of daunting distances and harassment by soldiers, offered the homesick people imprisonment at Keogh, a virtual return to their cherished place. How could Little Wolf refuse such an offer? And so march to the Fort they did, and there, after much resistance, Little Wolf and some of his men agreed to serve as scouts for Nelson Miles in an ongoing campaign against renegade Indians, an agreement that would help secure a reservation for the Northern Cheyenne.

Dull Knife, meanwhile, angled northwest from the Platte toward Fort Robinson in Nebraska, believing he could find provisions and a reprieve from want. The soldiers made his decision to stay at the fort easy, for they initially provided food and shelter. Yet these cold hosts came to insist that Dull Knife return to Indian Territory, simply an impossibility for the people who had traveled so far and sensed how close they were to familiar country. When the military turned surly, peremptory, insolent, demanding the return south, the Cheyenne informed the Army officers that they would only return as corpses. The soldiers adopted the cruelest of tactics, denying all food to the people. Once again starving and heartsick, the Cheyenne broke out from Fort Robinson, though it proved a bloody, awful affair: "Of about 150 Cheyennes who had been confined in the barracks up to this time, 64 were killed in the outbreak, about 58 were sent to Pine Ridge, about 20 to the south, while 8 or 10 were never again heard of, and no doubt were killed or starved to death in the hills." Yet most of those who survived did return to their homeland, a victory in the midst of apparent defeat.

Though classified as prisoners, the Northern Cheyenne "confined" at Fort Keogh were granted land along the Tongue River and Rosebud Creek south of Miles Town, in part out of practical necessity: The U. S. military could not continue to provision them when land was available for the taking. Yet, as the settlers' complaint in 1889 makes clear, not all Americans agreed with this strategy. In settlers' eyes, much of that land had already been claimed by emigrants, and moreover, in their view, the Cheyenne were not adopting the agrarian life that land was supposed to encourage and sustain. Increasing conflicts over grazing, cattle depredations (real or imagined), and confused encounters made it imperative to determine, once and for all, whether the Cheyenne would occupy land coveted by ranchers and Miles Town boosters, not to mention railroad magnates. After considerable debate in the nation's capital about how to settle this nagging issue on the far-off northern plains, on November 26, 1884, President Chester Arthur signed an executive order setting aside 256,000 acres for exclusive use by the Northern Cheyenne.

The petition to President Harrison that appears in May 1889 demonstrates that five years later many settlers simply do not accept the issue as resolved. None other than General Nelson Miles, the very namesake for the central town in the controversy, will step forth to refute the petition. In a letter dated June 1, 1889, and addressed to R. L. Upshaw, agent on the Tongue River Reservation, Miles recalls how the Cheyenne people aided his efforts as scouts and insists as well, with notable commonsense, that forcing a people to inhabit an entirely alien climate seems impractical and cruel:

> . . . in regard to the proposed removal of the Indians, I
> would say that, in my judgment, there is no good reason
> or justice in doing so. . . . During the last twelve years

they have been entirely peaceable. . . [T]he Government
had allowed them a little corner of territory upon which
to live, and justice, and humanity, and every other com-
mendable reason demands that they should be allowed
to live there. There is no reason why Indians can not be
well treated and allowed to live in peace in the vicinity in
which they were born.

One of the lingering paradoxes of this troubled in-between
time for indigenous peoples is how often the very military com-
manders who punished them so ruthlessly would advocate for
allowing those very "hostiles" to settle on land of their choosing.
Such a plea probably has as much to do with a sense of hon-
or—one must keep one's word—as with compassion or a deeper
sense of humanity, yet how striking to read the words of a fierce
warrior advocating for the Northern Cheyenne to remain on the
reservation created by executive order in 1884. Miles's words
will prove prophetic, for the Northern Cheyenne Reservation
will remain intact, and a follow-on executive order in 1900 will
confirm the native nation's right to this land.

JUNE

In which Granville Stuart falls in love, Havre begins, and a Cheyenne Sun Dance takes place.

———————

*Mr. John J. Kennedy of this city recently returned from Min-
nesota, where he purchased several hundred head of young
cattle. . . . Mr. Kennedy will place these cattle in the Milk river
country. . . . He says he has never seen a finer hay country
and that he could this season, if he wished, cut 5,000 tons of
unexcelled blue joint in that section.*

———————

G RANVILLE STUART IS IN LOVE. HE HAS FALLEN HARD
for a woman fully thirty years his junior, Allis Isabelle
Brown Fairfield. "Belle" had briefly served as schoolteacher for his children in the mid-1880s, and she returns like a
force of nature in 1889.

Awbonnie Tookanka Stuart, Granville's Shoshone wife, had
died the year before having given birth to 11 surviving children.
Awbonnie provided the emotional center of the large family, a
determined force who kept children and father together despite
the centrifugal energies of Granville's persistent scheming and
restlessness. As Teddy Blue Abbott, Stuart's future son-in-law,
will recall: "Being an Indian, she kept to herself when strangers
was around, and she wouldn't sit at the table with them or have
much to say, but she was a power in that family. And although
she caused Mary and me a lot of grief, I had to admire her just
the same because she made a wonderful wife and mother, and no
white woman could have raised those girls any better than she

Granville Stuart, 1883. PHOTOGRAPH BY L.A. HUFFMAN. MONTANA
HISTORICAL SOCIETY RESEARCH CENTER PHOTOGRAPH ARCHIVES, HELENA,
MONTANA

did. . . ." Stuart had been pressured by his mother and a changing Montana to abandon his first wife. A young Mary Ronan
penned a memorable portrait of the "scholarly" Stuart and the
moccasined Awbonnie in Virginia City in the mid-1860s, calling into question the fitness, the propriety of such a match. To
his credit, Stuart resisted those pressures and remained married
to Awbonnie until her death. His tribute upon her passing suggests the emotional and ethical bonds joining the couple:

> And now let the birds sing above her, the
> flowers bloom over her head, and the sighing
> winds gather their fragrance over our loved
> and lost. Noble, devoted, self-sacrificing wife,
> gentle and loving mother, Farewell.

With their strong mother gone, the Stuart family begins to
come undone. That unraveling accelerates with the unexpected
death of Granville and Awbonnie's oldest daughter, Katie, a special favorite of the father's and the logical new mother figure.
Perhaps the jarring losses of wife and daughter, along with his
own mother's death in November of 1888, lead Stuart to seek
solace and a new start. He turns to Belle, and the children drift
away from a father increasingly distracted by romance with a
white woman carrying a checkered past. After teaching for a
brief spell at the Stuarts' DHS Ranch, Belle seems to have attended a normal school in Indiana, before returning to Montana
to take up teaching duties in Sidney. A request to Granville to
serve as a reference for a teaching position at Fort Peck leads to
a proposal of marriage from the 55-year-old widower: "I know
twenty or more young women that would make good teachers
for Indian schools but I know of but one girl that would make
me a good wife. I will take you home and we will be married."
    Granville's opinionated daughter Mary does not spare her fa-
ther's love interest when she learns of the young woman's pres-

ence on the Stuart ranch less than a week after Katie's death. She writes to her fiancé Teddy Blue: "The teacher is the girl that Will Burnett run with when she taught school here her name was Belle Brown but now it is Mrs. Fairfield, but I don't think she was ever married you know what she was don't you I am surprised that papa got her but guess it is for his benefit don't you. well, Ted she is very pretty but did you ever see one that was't." The status of Belle's first marriage has never been fully established, so perhaps Mary's suspicions about Mr. Fairfield are not far-fetched. In any case, the oldest living daughter cannot suffer the presence of the intended.

Though rumor holds that Granville and Belle married as early as June of 1889, their official public wedding will take place January 8 of the following year. The oldest children separate from their father and his new wife, and the three youngest are sent to the St. Ignatius boarding school for Indian children, a surprising move given Granville's avowed and persistent resistance to formal religion.

Granville is called "Mr. Montana" for a reason—he lived out many of the changes to the place unfolding from the 1850s to the 1880s. Highly intelligent and well read, Granville is forever seeking the key to wealth, believing in his bones his talents deserve monetary reward. He and his beloved older brother, James, arrived in the Beaverhead Valley the fall of 1857 and cast their lot with this remote, beautiful land. Deer Lodge became their home base, and they tried a variety of means to secure wealth: gold mining at nearby Gold Creek, running cattle from the Oregon Trail, operating stores for miners at Bannack and Virginia City, exploring the Yellowstone River valley for gold and homesteads, and much more. Granville will memorably express his frustration that these diverse efforts yielded little: "It is awful to think how many d—d fools & asses are wallowing in wealth without any effort on their part to make it while we who could appreciate it & use it cant possibly make a cent." Devoted reader, student of nature, artist, and connoisseur of fine things, Granville may well have been a better dreamer and schemer than a doer.

In 1880, his brother James having died seven years earlier and his fortunes declining in Helena as he served as an accountant at Samuel Hauser's bank, Stuart jumped to another seemingly can't-fail opportunity: creating a cattle operation in central Montana. He used the spring of that year to tour the Judith, Musselshell, and Yellowstone valleys, seeking the most promising range for a massive herd. Stuart partnered with Hauser, Andrew Davis from Butte, and Andrew's brother Erwin Davis to bring a herd to the plains for breeding, fattening, and shipping. The partners were flush with the same hopefulness and greed articulated by James Brisbin in *The Beef Bonanza; or, How to Get Rich on the Plains*. They anticipated the arrival of the Northern Pacific Railroad to ship livestock to the processing center of Chicago, while fearing competition from eastern and European capital on the Montana range. The principle was the same as practiced time and again in early Montana: Get there first and exploit the natural advantages afforded by this newly available land.

Granville's journal of his search for prime rangeland provides an uncanny echo of his brother's 1863 journey to the Bighorn River in quest for a gold strike and a chance to build a town in yet-unclaimed land (that is, unclaimed by Americans—the Apsáalooke would point out they lived there). Granville's 1880 tour suggested a still-mourning brother not just retracing James's steps but seeking the means to redeem that failed expedition. His longing became clear in his effort to find his brother's signature written on the landscape: "Went down the river twelve miles and camped at noon in the forks of the Yellowstone and Big Horn rivers for the purpose of looking for my brother James's name, which with date he carved in the sandstone cliff between the rivers, when on the Yellowstone expedition 1863." While Granville located names for other members of the expedition, he did not find James's, a poignant reminder of the brother's failed quest. The earlier exploratory effort had ended in disaster as the Crows attacked James's party, killing two and wounding seven. None other than Samuel Hauser was part of that expedition and would live to tell tales of his own wounding and trauma. Perhaps, then, Granville not only longed to recover that ground but to prove that James's efforts, repeated with similarly futile results in 1864, were not for naught. Perhaps a younger brother could make good on the promise of that dream from 17 years earlier. Perhaps James's leadership and those deaths could be made to yield profit and a good life after all.

That desire for brotherly redemption could help explain Granville's decision to pursue grazing rights on the Crow reservation in the Little Bighorn Valley. He saw this setting as ideal for his ranch, the valley lush with grass, well watered, and sheltered. But negotiations with the Crow did not go well, and so Stuart returned to the Judith Basin, an area already being ranched by James Fergus, an old friend from early territorial days, and the legendary DHS Ranch was born.

Granville's quest for the next best opportunity did not take place in a vacuum, of course. He covered contested ground, reservation boundaries and hunting areas still very much in dispute among the native nations and the re-United States that coveted the land. Stuart often observed hunting parties from the Piegan, Crow, and Lakota nations, as well as the mobile Métis. His anger reached genocidal proportions when he wrote to Hauser in July, 1881, "If we can obtain our rights in no other way than through an Indian war, war it shall be, for I will not stand idly by, & be mocked in this manner, while our property is being destroyed by these thieving murderous savages." In less incendiary moments, Stuart advocated for the allotment system that would force each Indian to claim 160 acres and convert to an agricultural life. In Stuart's eyes this would be the most humane treatment for people unwilling or unable to adapt to a new reality, a new world, one dictated by the expansive, powerful United

Heating branding irons on Granville Stuart's DHS Ranch, Judith Basin, 1888.
Montana Historical Society Research Center Photograph Archives, Helena, Montana

States, one that should provide Stuart the financial security he so clearly craved.

Yet to his credit, during his tour Stuart took note of dire changes to the land, such as in his shocked account of bison destruction:

> From the Porcupine clear to Miles City the bottoms are liberally sprinkled with the carcasses of dead buffalo. In many places they lie thick on the ground, fat and the meat not yet spoiled, all murdered for their hides which are piled like cord wood all along the way. 'Tis an awful sight. Such a waste of the finest meat in the world! Probably ten thousand buffalo have been in this vicinity this winter. Slaughtering the buffalo was a government measure to subjugate the Indians.

This passage seems a rebuke to Theodore Roosevelt's cavalier attitude toward extermination of the bison. Yet isn't there something disingenuous about this shock and horror? If the bison were not removed and the Indians confined, how could Stuart and his partners make a killing on the plains of Montana?

While conducting his inspection of potential cattle ranges, Stuart met two men representing the immediate past and the emerging future for Montana: "Left Miles City on the twenty-second [of April, 1880] at 11 A.M. and went up the river twenty-three miles to Anderson's ranch where we fell in with Yellow-stone Kelley (Luther S. Kelley). . . [and] an L. A. Huffman, a young photographer from Fort Keogh." Kelly was the famous hunter and scout who had arrived in Montana in 1866 after being discharged from the Union Army. He became an authority on the plains and valleys east of Montana's continental divide, a strikingly handsome man so renowned for his knowledge that he served as chief scout for Nelson Miles during the campaign against the Nez Perce in 1877. Miles will write the glowing foreword to Kelly's memoirs, asserting ". . .there appeared a most in-

teresting character, equally as fearless, intelligent, and resourceful as Daniel Boone, David Crockett, Kit Carson, or William F.
Cody. His name was Luther S. Kelly but he was better known as
'Yellowstone Kelly.' . . . [H]e explored that extensive northwest
country years before serious hostilities occurred and acquired
a knowledge of its topography, climate, and resources that was
exceedingly valuable."

While Kelly's time in Montana soon came to an end as he
headed for Colorado, Huffman was a recent arrival, one whom
Stuart clearly valued: "Huffman is one of the most companion-
able men I ever traveled with." Huffman left Iowa for a chance to
record a fast-disappearing West through his photographic art.
His images provide a critical, affecting lens on the Indians and
cowboys who inhabited Montana in the 1880s. He will return
Stuart's praise and produce one of the very best portraits of Mr.
Montana, and he will purchase some of Evelyn Cameron's stunning photographs. Huffman will also become a close friend of
that iconic Montana cowboy, Charles M. Russell.

As for Granville's making a killing through cattle ranching,
he went deep into debt investing in the DHS Ranch and saw
decreasing dividends for the owners as the 1880s unfolded.
Ironically, almost in spite of these financial struggles, he took
on increased stature as a leading citizen of the Territory, serving
as leader of the Montana Stockgrowers Association, representing the Montana ranges at national gatherings of cattle outfits,
and, most notoriously, organizing the vigilante effort that strung
up at least 20 accused horse thieves. These vigilantes would be
forever known as Stuart's Stranglers, a title Stuart would never
publicly claim but which seemed to state accurately his role in
the proceedings. Not only did the Stranglers repeat many of the
extralegal mistakes made by the more famous vigilantes of the
gold camps, but they frequently focused on individuals with
mixed-race backgrounds, suggesting more than economic interests may have been at play in these lynchings.

Whatever his reputation and standing, in the spring of 1887 Stuart was fired as superintendent of the DHS. A letter from Percy Kennett to his stepfather, Hauser, provided the pretext for replacing the long-time Montanan:

> Granville himself is all right in his present position, but the location of the ranch is wrong, it is too near the Fort & Maiden, as I say Granville is a good Supt, but I cannot run a ranch & have to hire his half breed relatives or have they & their friends around and do it economically. There is too many girls on this ranch, & I am satisfied now that Reece Anderson just lives off the Co. One cannot put anything around & have it long. The boys seem to think that everything here, they are entitled to have. I am satisfied that I can run the outfit several thousand dollars cheaper a year than it has ever been run. I do not want to run Granville out of his position, & if you want me to I can resign. But the outfit will never be run very cheap as long as you have to support his boys & Reece Andersons family.

When Stuart falls hard for Belle, then, he has suffered both familial and financial losses. He may have longed for a break from thirty years of striving and failing in Montana, a chance to begin anew, to take on a new partner for life and turn toward new opportunities. If daughter Mary and her siblings resent Granville's choices, so be it. A man in his mid-50s, no matter how distinguished or respected, must find his way in the hit-or-miss, topsy-turvy economy of an almost-state in the isolated northwest. Niceties of mollifying hurt children may seem a secondary concern at this stage of his life.

WHO WOULDN'T PICK IT OUT FOR A HOMESTEAD, THE BOTTOMS of Bull Hook Creek, where the stream flows into the Milk River, covered by tall, rasping cottonwood trees, a place so natural the Indians camped here summer and fall? John Bell, who served his time at Fort Assinniboine, just to the south, built himself a cabin on the bottoms in 1887, claiming land not rightly belonging to him. But isn't possession nine-tenths of the law?

This has been country for the Cree and Chippewa, the Métis, the Gros Ventre and Assiniboine, and of course those pesky Blackfeet, but with Jim Hill's railroad driving through this country, those days are gone, long gone. The Sweetgrass Treaty and the right-of-way granted to the railroad mean no more wandering for the tribes. No, it's time they settle down on their land and let the white men put the country to use. Besides, that tyro Hill will surely build a depot here someday, no doubt about it, because the Montana Central will link up with the soon-to-be Great Northern right here.

Bell's modest place was joined by Simon Pepin's, an employee of Charles Broadwater's Diamond R Freighting Company, the summer of 1888, and then Gus Decelles' cabin appears this summer of 1889, and there you have it, the very makings of a town. A tent city springs up north and south of the tracks, and soon the biggest news of all: Hill will extend his transcontinental railroad due west from this very point, bypassing Great Falls, for one of his chief engineers has found the lowest pass through those Rocky Mountains, with a gentle slope on the eastern side, and logic and money dictate the line must now go straight from here.

But Mr. Hill will not stand for this key transit point on the Great Northern to be called "Bull Hook Bottoms," no siree. When it comes time to name a town in 1891, the citizens will assemble to attempt to agree on a proper moniker, and the result will be fist fights and bitter feelings. So Hill will ask the original settlers to choose a fitting name, and given their common French heritage, they will settle on "Havre," named for France's La Havre, the harbor or haven, a fitting name for this coming town on the railroad that will connect northern Montana to the great markets of the Midwest. What a fine thing. Havre. Has a

Fort Assinniboine, Montana, marching band and soldiers on parade ground, officers quarters in background, circa 1891. MONTANA HISTORICAL SOCIETY RESEARCH CENTER PHOTOGRAPH ARCHIVES, HELENA, MONTANA

ring to it. And a future. Of course, in its early days, it will draw the cowboys, soldiers, railroad workers, and wolfers, and so it will earn a reputation as a completely uncivilized town. But civilization comes to most towns in time, and Havre will become a fine, carefully gridded stopping point for those trains running west and east, connecting Minneapolis to Seattle, and Montana to the big world. Havre will be a node, a meeting point, a nexus. Havre will be a haven and a harbor, a place of landings and leavings.

JOHN STANDS IN TIMBER TELLS,

> I saw the last Sun Dance they put on seventy years ago [on the Northern Cheyenne Reservation]. It was just like dreaming, I saw that tepee. That makes it 1889—that must be about the time they stopped; they started it again in 1907, the first one, after I came back from school. I saw one down here at the mouth of Tie Creek, going along with my grandmother outside the camp; I just remember like waking up and seeing a big lodge. Then I don't remember.

JULY

In which Rudyard Kipling visits Livingston, Clara McAdow lobbies for women's suffrage during the Constitutional Convention, Lizzie Fisk eschews public meetings, Pierre Wibaux builds a cattle kingdom, and Samuel Hauser pleads for investors.

At noon to-day a deliberative body will come into being in this city which is certain to wield a great influence upon the destiny of the state of Montana. The men chosen to form a constitution for the new state have been selected quite as much for their recognized fitness for the work as for any political reputation they may have. . . . The best way for men in this convention to help their party is to labor for the good of the whole people.

RUDYARD KIPLING, 23, PAUSES ON HIS JOURNEY ACROSS America to record his impressions of Livingston on July 2, 1889. He is not yet the world-famous author of *The Jungle Book* who will receive the Nobel Prize for Literature in 1907. The son of British functionaries in India, Kipling composes this article for an Indian newspaper to help pay his way home to England. He had disembarked at San Francisco, traveled up the west coast to Oregon and Washington, then trained east to the jumping off point for the famous Yellowstone Park, created seventeen years earlier. In this way he reverses the usual flow of humanity and desire from east to west, consciously countering the forward thrust of Manifest Destiny. This small, witty, gimlet-eyed visitor offers a decidedly mixed view of the emerging community:

> Livingston is a town of two thousand people, and the junction for the little side-line that takes you to the Yellowstone National Park. It lies in a fold of the prairie, and behind it is the Yellowstone River and the gate of the mountains through which the river flows. There is one street in the town, where the cowboy's pony and the little foal of the brood-mare in the buggy rest contentedly in the blinding sunshine while the cowboy gets himself shaved at the only other barber's shop, and swaps lies at the bar. I exhausted the town, including the saloons, in ten minutes, and got away on the rolling grass downs where I threw myself to rest. . . . In every bar-room lay a copy of the local paper, and every copy impressed it upon the inhabitants of Livingston that they were the best, finest, bravest, richest, and most progressive town of the most progressive nation under Heaven. . . . They raise horses and minerals round and about Livingston, but they behave as though they raised cherubims with diamonds in their wings.

Kipling's hilarious, condescending portrait of a new Western town is of a piece with his larger critique of the raw American West. In his newspaper articles, he returns often to naïve American boosterism, exaggeration of status and style, and unbridled confidence in national exceptionalism. Writing as a scion of the British Empire, confident of its excellence and the virtue imparted by established institutions and cultural norms, Kipling finds American cocksureness particularly laughable. His satire only takes on added bite with the approach of the Fourth of July, a celebration guaranteed to bring out the most extreme form of American jingoism.

Kipling does take that trip to Yellowstone Park, but not before spending time with the famous Yankee Jim, inspiring one of the sardonic visitor's most memorable descriptions. "[A] picturesque old man with a talent for yarns," the Montana host provokes Kipling to tell a few whoppers himself, but "Yankee Jim saw every one of my tales and went fifty better on the spot. He dealt in bears and Indians—never less than twenty of each; had known the Yellowstone country for years; and bore upon his body marks of Indian arrows." Fortunately, the famous canyon named for Jim yields a fine cache of trout, and a local woman catches the young writer's ever-attentive eye. An evening in Paradise Valley proves a delight after all.

As for the famous wonderland south of Gardiner, "To-day I am in the Yellowstone Park, and I wish I were dead." Kipling is caught in the vortex of Gilded Age American tourists, a type frequently skewered by Mark Twain and other humorists. The sharp contrast between the natural wonders of the park—the Grand Canyon of the Yellowstone evokes one of Kipling's most gorgeous lyrical passages—and the garrulous, obtuse tourists from the eastern United States brings out the dyspeptic Kipling. Since he launches upon the park tour on the Fourth, behind horses covered with American flags pulling his touring car, the occasion only intensifies the pain. Kipling reveals how Yellowstone has already become an international wonder, the attractor of the rich and famous, one of the go-to spots for members of the emerging upper class to see and be seen. Indeed, the Livingston newspaper Kipling mentions scathingly includes an article about Henry Villard, king of the Northern Pacific Railroad, traveling to the park with a large party on his luxurious train car over the Fourth. Yellowstone is an economic engine, a symbol, a magnet, and it's one reason Livingston appears a surer bet for success than Billings in 1889.

Kipling's insight into the western United States goes beyond the easy sarcasm apparent in his quick takes on Livingston and

Yellowstone. He is perceptive about an important check on American ambition: "the great American nation . . . very seldom attempts to put back anything that it has taken from Nature's shelves. It grabs all it can and moves on. But the moving-on is nearly finished and the grabbing must stop." In a sense the British newspaperman anticipates Turner's frontier thesis, which will be delivered four years later at the Columbian Exposition, but Kipling sees the end of the frontier less as a crisis of national identity and more as an opportunity to face the responsibility and hard choices imposed by limits of space and time.

CLARA MCADOW GREETS EACH AND EVERY DELEGATE TO THE convention—many are friends or acquaintances, met through her mining business, or during her salad days in Billings, or through her husband, Perry "Bud" McAdow, an old-time pioneer who has been in Montana since before it was a territory. Clara feels it's her right to step up and greet them, encourage them to support women's right to vote in this new constitution they're writing. Let them include this simple clause in the document that will determine Montana's future: "All citizens 21 years of age, of sound mind, not convicted of crime, shall have the right of suffrage irrespective of sex."

Clara has surely heard some of those voices, those naysayers calling her brash and unladylike, accosting these gentlemen with her views on the mental capacity of women, the need for wives and mothers and daughters to have their say in how their new state will be governed. In the critics' eyes she is just a harridan, or worse, beyond the pale of respectability, loud and boisterous. Those back-biters might even mouth that old nickname "Captain Tom," a reference to her first husband's name, Tomlinson, and to her commanding presence as a woman of property in Billings. But Clara has lived enough—spent time enough with men and women in Michigan and Montana and many points in between—to know that women have as much capacity as men,

Clara L. McAdow. Montana Historical Society Research Center Photograph Archives, Helena, Montana

P. W. McAdow, taken when he was a delegate to the Montana Constitutional Convention, 1889. Montana Historical Society Research Center Photograph Archives, Helena, Montana

and more to the point, have as much at stake in those political decisions. Who better to know the cost of legislation about mining, ranching, schools, prisons, and all the rest than the very people who witness the loss and gain on a daily basis in the political economy of home and business?

She surely does not mean to challenge the courage and tenacity of men like Bud, an exceptional fellow in his own way, despite being confined to a wheelchair by a mysterious paralysis. He advocates for women's suffrage as well, a sure sign of respect for the misnamed "fairer sex." He even introduced the idea during the 1884 Constitutional Convention, that failed effort to make a state. Clara and Bud met on the Yellowstone River in 1883 after Mr. Tomlinson's passing. When her first husband, a physician, asked that they move west to the dry plains to cure his suffering lungs, Clara doubted. Leaving green Michigan for sere Montana was not her idea of paradise, yet something caught her when they landed in that would-be town of Coulsen. Maybe it was the Yellowstone River, the thought of those waters flowing out of the majestic mountains to the west, the link to the Missouri, the connection to the Mississippi. Maybe it was simply that opportunity stood forth, called her name. Coulsen and Huntly and Billings and those other new river towns breathed real estate, something Clara knew well, and with the Northern Pacific Railroad driving through, she guessed that disorganized outfit would need common sense. So she clerked for the railroad and started buying up land. Sadly, her dear first husband could not escape the fate he fled, and Bud turned his attentions to her. Clara assumes he caught sight of energy, gumption, and belief. Folks are puzzled by their match, curious about the seeming coldness between them. Clara and Bud do not demonstrate their affection often, and perhaps they really are more like business partners than mates. They're both long in the tooth, of course, well past youth, so that cools the ardor. And Clara has become disillusioned with the old pioneer, caught up in a civil case brought by a former mistress claiming he'd promised to marry her. One hundred forty scandalous letters were entered into evidence, exposing Bud's folly to the wide, garrulous world. Clara can endure any number of challenges to her dignity, but that exposure has ended hopes for a permanent partnership. Clara has already established a prominent home in Michigan with the proceeds from their joint enterprises, and once this convention ends, she'll assume an independent life there.

So perhaps it is with a combination of nostalgia and regret that Clara recalls those times they sat by the Yellowstone River on warm evenings in their first years together, Bud smoking the pipe, her working the knitting needles, and reminisced about his time in this wild place. He arrived early, 1861, got the jump on Gold Creek and Bannack and Alder Gulch, made a fair amount of money, then he threw his fortunes in with that schemer John Bozeman, built a mill in the Gallatin with the man who would murder Bozeman, Tom Cover, and realized mining the miners was far more lucrative and less back-breaking than working the claims. Besides, the easy pickings were played out. Why not create something to last, not the quick strike and move to the next dig, but property and buildings and his name on a sign? Yet lucrative as the town of Bozeman proved, Bud couldn't stop thinking about the Yellowstone country, there for the picking, save for those Crows and Sioux and Cheyenne, perfect bottomlands for farming and ranching, a sure water and shipping source, and the railroad, the thing that would change everything, was following the river's course. He had his terrible times on the Yellowstone back in the 1860s, when he was attacked and nearly killed by marauding Sioux, but if a man couldn't get the jump, he couldn't claim the best land and the best prospects.

So Bud took the contract to supply beef and flour to the Crow in 1877, and that was the leap across the divide that changed his life. That very summer the Nez Perce came through that country during their flight to Canada, and they murdered and burned.

Bud had his doubts about the wisdom of staying put in a place so changeable and subject to chance, and the Indians were by no means tamed just a year after Custer's fall. He always had that itch, though, that need to build something, test, try. He would get restless when he was too comfortable. So it was his trading post in a tent, and claiming land, and dreaming of a mighty city on that pretty river.

Bud threw in with the very town he named, Coulsen, and it looked like he would make a killing when the railroad passed right through his investments. But the railroad had a mind of its own, and so Billings was birthed by NPRR's running its line there. After the initial shock, Bud and Clara and others got in on the ground floor with buying up property in the new town, in some ways easy pickings but a gamble after all. And in truth, looking at Billings these days, Clara must have her occasional doubts it will become the city those early arrivals imagined. It looks a bit bedraggled and downtrodden, eclipsed by towns like Miles and Livingston. But if a person considers all the natural advantages, that beautiful river valley, the Crow and Cheyenne nearby needing supplies, she has to believe it will rise one day.

Life took yet another turn for Clara and Bud when he found a mine in Maiden, up in the Judith Mountains. That eminent man, Granville Stuart, called it "the biggest mine in Montana." Bud had so many friends who would pass along news, and he found out about this promising outfit about a hundred miles north of Billings. When he bought it up, the shaft ran 60 feet and yielded good gold, though there was only a small rolling mill to bring it out. That's when Clara's mind went to work. Bud was in terrible health, perhaps reminding her of Mr. Tomlinson, and so he sought a cure in California. What choice did Clara have but to manage the mine? They called it Spotted Horse, and it became her peculiar project, her pet, her satisfaction. Think how primitive the place was, no roads, no outfitters, no mill, just a shaft in the ground that showed promise of wealth.

Clara's mind liked organizing things, putting together puz-
zles. She told Bud if he established the contacts and helped re-
cruit the men, she'd ride herd on this mine. So Clara built those
roads, built that mill, and recruited the suppliers. Of course
those rough men were shocked at first, and reluctant to work
for a woman. It seemed a real come-down for them. Once again,
that phrase "Captain Tom" started circulating. Yet every time
they asked her a question, Clara had an answer, and she paid
good wages. Never missed a pay day. Maybe living in a town
called Maiden helped her cause. Besides, women have as much
intelligence and will as men, only they've learned to hide it in
a thousand ways. What a waste of energy and talent, all these
brilliant ladies channeling their abilities into make-believe lives
dedicated to socializing and appearances.

It is with high anticipation, then, that Clara sits in the gallery
in the courthouse, front row, as usual, to hear Mr. Henry Blackwell from Massachusetts deliver his talk on women's suffrage
before the Constitutional Convention on a warm July night,
fanning herself, a fluttering of nerves and hope. Bud and Clara
recruited Mr. Blackwell for the task and know his speech nearly
verbatim. Their advocate proclaims that the Enabling Legislation demands adherence to the stirring words of the Declaration
of Independence: "We hold these truths to be self-evident, that
all men are created equal, that they are endowed by their Creator with certain inalienable Rights, that among these are Life,
Liberty, and the pursuit of Happiness." Is it not self-evident that
women are born with these rights as much as any being? And
note, Mr. Blackwell continues, how Americans have extended
the right to vote throughout their history, first to men without
property in Andrew Jackson's time, then to the Negro in Lincoln's time. History is progressive. Surely women must be next.
And what of women's qualifications to participate in civic life?
While they have As much or more at stake in political decisions,
they carry different qualities that make them especially fit to ex-

ercise their civic duty: Women are less subject to gross vices, less governed by base passion, more peaceable, more temperate. While Clara may have found this section of the speech layered on a bit thick, having witnessed many a woman who defies these generalizations (think of Calamity Jane, for instance, a frequent guest on the Yellowstone), on the whole that argument holds. And again, isn't it simply just to extend this fundamental right to half the species? Besides, Montana women have participated in school elections already, and as best anyone can tell, no catastrophe has ensued.

Still, Clara's cause remains a long bet. For all the ardent support of Bud and noble men like Judge Knowles from Butte, Martin Maginnis and Joseph Toole, powerful, popular politicians, remain adamantly opposed, and their arguments will likely carry the day with more feckless delegates. Their ace in the hole: Women's suffrage might sink the vote in favor of the constitution, delaying Montana's statehood yet again. A clever plea, to be sure. Yet Clara will not give up—it is not in her nature. Perhaps her advocacy is given an extra jolt, an extra electricity from her being humiliated by Bud's very public affairs, that sense her dignity as an independent woman has been demeaned. So she continues to buttonhole the delegates, greet them with her direct gaze and firm words, compel them to look her in the eye and tell her why they are opposed to simple justice. And yes, she sits in the front row of the visitors' area every day, leaning forward, making her presence felt. She will not stop advocating, for it is a woman's right to participate fully in Montana's elections. Her life is proof positive of that self-evident truth.

LIZZIE FISK WRITES HER MOTHER ON THE 7TH DAY OF JULY, expressing distaste for active political involvement by women even as the Montana Constitutional Convention settles in for its seven-week session in her hometown of Helena:

Elizabeth Chester Fisk, photograph taken in the early 1860s. MONTANA HISTORICAL SOCIETY RESEARCH CENTER PHOTOGRAPH ARCHIVES, HELENA, MONTANA

Like you, I wonder how ladies find time for so many
societies. Though a member of the W.C.T.U. I never attend the meetings. They have for a long time been held
on Saturday afternoon, a time when I cannot well leave
home. While I approve the temperance and reformatory
work of the organization, I do object very strongly to the
action of some of its leaders in attempting to commit the
members to the third party movement. . . . It may be right
for women who have no children and few home cares to
attend meetings constantly and work for the public. Those
who have families certainly cannot do it.

The letter communicates the ambiguities and uncertain-
ties accompanying a prominent middle-class wife and mother
taught a stern Connecticut faith in a woman's role as spiritual
guide, companion, and nurturer. A lifelong Republican sure of
the justice of abolitionism and the Union cause, Lizzie married
a Civil War leader and member of the prominent Fisk family,
the very family that produced James, famous for leading emigrants out of Minnesota (including such central early settlers
as Nathaniel Langford and James Fergus) along the Northern
Overland Route.

When she arrived in Montana with her husband, Robert, in
1867, Lizzie met the shock of a new mining town with bravado,
hopefulness, and a fair amount of New England squeamishness.
As Robert established himself in the newspaper trade by editing
and publishing an important Republican-leaning newspaper,
the *Helena Weekly Herald*, Lizzie tentatively tested the limits of
propriety for a respectable woman in the wide open town that
featured saloons, brothels, and gambling houses. Once her six
children began arriving, however, she recommitted to the domestic ideal inculcated by Victorian American culture. Since
she often sent letters to her mother, she left behind an unusually
rich, frank account of such a woman's life in a remote territory.

Main Street in Helena, Montana, looking north from Bridge Street, circa 1879.
Montana Historical Society Research Center Photograph Archives, Helena, Montana

Main Street in Helena, Montana, looking south from Sixth Avenue, circa 1891.
MONTANA HISTORICAL SOCIETY RESEARCH CENTER PHOTOGRAPH ARCHIVES, HEL-
ENA, MONTANA

The letter she writes in early July reveals her mixed emotions about political engagement in the territorial capital city. She confirms her commitment to the Women's Christian Temperance Union, a nationwide movement to curtail drinking, especially by men, toward the goal of improving both men's and women's lives. A non-drinker herself, Lizzie was instrumental in starting the Montana branch of WCTU in 1883, and in fact had been elected a regional representative. Yet she has grown increasingly uneasy with the organization's tilt toward imposing prohibition on Montana, a stance too strong for a moderate Republican who prefers the more pragmatic action of encouraging temperance pledges by individuals. Perhaps even more importantly, the letter's allusion to WCTU's leaders "attempting to commit the members to the third party movement" refers to an infusion of advocates for the Populist Party, which in Lizzie's eyes advocates radical measures such as women's rights and addressing disparities in wealth. Perhaps with more rationalization than sincere reason, Lizzie claims her status as mother and wife prevents her from attending many public events, especially on Saturdays dedicated to caring for her children, home from school, and to meeting her social obligation to entertain guests.

Yet Fisk's ambivalence here should not be taken to signal a withdrawal from struggles for social justice. Just the year before, she had been elected president of the Women's Relief Corps, dedicated to aiding poor women in need, and the year before that, she served as a trustee for the newly created Women's Home Incorporated, formed "to assist working women to secure employment and to furnish a home to those who may desire to avail themselves of the same." Especially concerned about the welfare of women in the growing town, aware of profound changes introduced by the arrival of the railroads that made travel to Helena that much easier for a cross-section of Americans, and cognizant of the extreme disparities in wealth in her hometown (Helena could claim 50 millionaires in 1890, the highest number per capita in the United States), Fisk steps up to assist marginalized, lonely, vulnerable women. In this way, she demonstrates how social institutions emerge in nascent communities, often through the volunteer labor of women who cannot participate formally in civic life by holding office or voting. Yet as a product of New England idealism and middle-class codes, she cannot take the leap to full-on political engagement embodied by the likes of Clara McAdow. Her letters suggest there may well be a personal dimension to this uncertainty. Time and again, Lizzie Fisk plunges into a cause only to withdraw after a time of intense involvement. Her rigid Connecticut values may cause her to judge her fellow advocates harshly, her idealism a check on her pragmatism, her ability to cooperate fully with others who do not meet her standards.

Perhaps this personal squeamishness about flawed human beings accounts for one of Fisk's haunting acts of prejudice. Helen Clarke, the charismatic daughter of Malcolm Clarke, a key factor for the American Fur Company and builder of a ranch north of Helena, and his Piegan wife, Coth-co-co-na, served as a teacher in Helena during the 1880s. Lizzie Fisk withdrew her children from school in protest of Clarke's role:

> I do not intend sending Grace and Robbie [her two oldest children] to school again this winter. . . . I have long been dissatisfied with the school. Mr. [R.J.] Howie, the Principal, is an excellent Christian man. Grace's teacher, Miss Clark, is a half-breed Indian, the daughter of Malcolm Clark, who, you perhaps remember, was killed by the Indians nearly eleven years ago. Miss C. was educated in a convent and is avowedly a Catholic, but she has no faith in God or man. She hates the school, hates her work. While I am sorry for her, she is not the person I would choose as an instructor of my children.

Pierre Wibaux, 1900. Montana Historical Society Research Center Photograph Archives, Helena, Montana

Such attitudes help explain why Helen Clarke flees Helena in 1889, determined to find work outside her home state.

HE IS ONE OF THE NEW MEN, PIERRE WIBAUX, AND HE IS BUILD-ing a fortune on the backs of cattle at a time when old hands, such as Granville Stuart, flee ranching. On July 11, he ships a trainload of cattle to Chicago for processing, and follows with another load on July 19. His stock is reported to be of high quality, with steers averaging 1,325 pounds and bringing $3.65 per hundredweight. Wibaux has not just survived the catastrophic winter of 1886-1887, he uses it as the means to accumulate wealth. Following the devastating winter, he can acquire neighboring ranches' stock at reduced prices, so that even a relatively low rate for his steers in Chicago yields a tidy profit. Earlier in 1889, for instance, with money borrowed from his father, he acquired the entire herd of the renowned Powder River Cattle Company, 10,000 head, contributing to his total herd of 65,000 by the mid-90s. No wonder he establishes the W Bar Ranch, complete with a beautiful "White House" for his family, twelve miles north of the town that will soon bear his name.

Wibaux is not just a new man, he is a foreign man, and one who realizes the potential of the much-touted beef bonanza in Montana. Among all the colorful expats who inhabit or invest in Montana, Wibaux will turn out to be one of the most modern, capable, and effective capitalists. Born in France in 1858 into a family of successful textile manufacturers, he seems to have entered the world with an acute mind for business. During an informational tour of textile factories in England, he caught wind of money to be made in the cattle business on the plains of America. Unlike many an emigrant who arrived in the region more hopeful than keen, Wibaux carefully studied the cattle industry during his journey to his new home, stopping in Chicago to examine the trade as a total process, seeking to understand the raising, processing, and selling of beef. He realized early that

Pierre Wibaux's W Bar cattle on water. PHOTOGRAPH BY L.A. HUFFMAN. MONTANA HISTORICAL SOCIETY RESEARCH CENTER PHOTOGRAPH ARCHIVES, HELENA, MONTANA

he must anticipate the demands and tastes of his buyers. And make no mistake, Wibaux recognized his cattle operation would be part of an industrial system. His beef bonanza would only be possible with the arrival of the Northern Pacific along the Yellowstone River, the lifeline leading directly to the Chicago processing plants. That's why he induces the railroad to build stockyards in his new community on the Montana/Dakota border. The French businessman shows the incorporation of Montana into national and international markets through the nitty-gritty processes of stock raising and shipping.

Once he went all in with Montana in 1883, Wibaux claimed land with a partner and spent three years as a true cowboy on the range, roughing it and learning the rituals, trials, and potential of ranching. A letter home suggested the character of the man: "In other words it is a funny life; always ready to go, no matter what we eat, where we sleep, or what our existence. Still I am not worried. You know how much I love comfort and an easy life, and how long I have lived idly. I can't understand myself now. I have to look forward and no dangers, privations, or deceptions can draw me back. My luck and my love is my future. I am engaged in a contest and I will return victoriously." He carefully sited his operation, not only concerned about proximity to the rail line but attentive to weather patterns that could threaten his livestock. He chose land in the Beaver Creek Valley that provided maximum shelter from wind and moisture. He also grows his own hay to feed his cattle, not relying on the public domain that was becoming badly overgrazed. He employs, as well, wolfers to patrol for animals that could reduce his herd, his profit.

Given his evident intelligence and Old World connections, it is not surprising that Wibaux befriended the likes of Teddy Roosevelt and the Marquis De Mores, one of the more memorable inhabitants of the Montana and Dakota plains in the late nineteenth century. Wibaux arrived at virtually the same moment as the grief-stricken Roosevelt, and on first blush, no one would have predicted the Frenchman would thrive while the New Yorker abandoned the plains. After all, TR had the backing of an elite eastern family's fortune, cultural familiarity, and unbridled optimism. But the combination of that brutal winter, overgrazed range, and changes to Roosevelt's personal life led him away from his temporary home on the Dakota plains. De Mores' woes were both more colorful and more predictable. Not for nothing was he called the "Crazy Frenchman." Legend tells that this fellow Frenchman encouraged Wibaux to claim land on the northern tier, when they apparently met in Chicago during Wibaux's exploratory visit in 1883. Their relationship could not always be described as friendly, for De Mores' wife will tell of a near-duel between the two during a heated argument. De Mores, it seems, was fond of such encounters. In any case, the two immigrants' business approaches provide a study in contrasts. De Mores was determined to build a vertically and horizontally integrated cattle operation, complete with stockyards in Medora, North Dakota (named for his wife), and restaurants in Manhattan. He dreamed of controlling beef from hoof to plate. He invested enormous wealth—his own and his wife's—in the enterprise, only to see it collapse. The railroads contributed to his downfall, refusing to offer good shipping rates for a business that could threaten their profits.

The *Daily Yellowstone Journal* summarizes the Marquis's career with a large dose of schadenfreude, no doubt contrasting his home town's trajectory with Miles City's:

> Medora had a short season of rapid growth when the charming French nobleman and rather visionary man of business, the Marquis de Mores, made it the seat of his slaughtering and beef shipping enterprise. The big abattoir is silent and deserted now, and is presumably the property of his creditors. The brick hotel is closed, and so

Samuel T. Hauser, 1884. Montana Historical Society Research Center Photograph Archives, Helena, Montana

is the Marquis' chateau on the hill and there is small use for the brick church he built.

No wonder Wibaux has few illusions about the means to money in the cattle industry—De Mores' spectacular failure provided a vivid life lesson just as Wibaux set about developing his ranching operation.

SAMUEL HAUSER, MONTANA MAGNATE, IS BULLISH ON THE gold mines at Pony. He sends an effusive letter to Frederick Billings and other potential backers on July 11 encouraging investment in this complex of presumably mineral-rich tunnels:

> I feel it is just and right that you should have the opportunity to subscribe under the new bond, if you feel like taking the risk. . . . I can only say that all mining ventures are risky, that we will all probably make a big killing, or lose all we put in. . . . If the prospect is worth anything, it is worth twenty times what we put in. I am going to put my money in and take chances, and each and every dollar goes in on the same terms as mine.

Hauser is at the height of his wealth and power, an ever-active schemer for mines, railroads, banks, irrigation projects, and more. He arrived in 1862 onboard the same riverboat, the *Emilie*, that had carried such notable characters as Francis Thompson, an important witness to Montana's creation as a territory, and the James Vail family, missionaries committed to serving at the Sun River Indian Farm, only to see their lives go smash when Electa Bryan, Vail's sister-in-law, married Henry Plummer a mere eight months before his hanging at Bannack. Hauser left behind a respectable career as a civil engineer for Missouri railroads because his pro-Southern views put him at odds with his pro-Union family during the first years of the Civil War. Like so many of those landing in the place about to be transformed into the Territory of Montana, Hauser fled martial and familial conflict for a chance at a new start.

Hauser is often characterized as small, energetic, talkative, likable. He must have been hyper-active, for trying to track the many business opportunities pursued during his relatively long life could prove exhausting. Certainly one of the most dramatic was the legendary journey in the spring of 1863 to the Big Horn River with James Stuart. Hauser joined a party committed to opening country long dominated by the Crow but very much contested by the Lakota and Cheyenne. Stuart's expedition dreamed of building a city at the mouth of the Big Horn, thereby controlling traffic along the Yellowstone and the cut-off from the Oregon Trail that would become known as the Bozeman Trail. They were also pursuing gold, a belief only reinforced by finding color on the lower Bighorn.

The indigenous peoples who claimed the place as home would not stand for this overt act of appropriation. Sam Hauser was lucky to live to tell the tale. In one of those intergenerational connections that recur in a place with a relatively small population, such that prominent citizens often know each other, Frank Linderman will share a remarkable story of Sam Hauser recounting the deadly attack on Stuart's party. Since Linderman will guide Hauser on hunting trips in the 1890s, he will have occasion to hear the tale straight from the great man during one of those campfire revelations:

> Sitting by our fire [he] told me the whole story of that terrible experience, of the night attack by Indians who had followed them for days, of the awfulness of the moments when, according to agreement, several of their wounded comrades killed themselves, and the final escape of the rest of the party. The Governor, wrought up by his remembrances, walked, even ran, about the fire showing,

in pantomime, many unwritten details too revolting to record.

Hauser's career raises the fascinating question of why some early Montana capitalists ascended to unknown heights of wealth (think Daly, Clark, and A.B. Hammond of Missoula), while others climbed partway, only to fall. Given his energy, connections, and Democratic loyalty in a territory dominated by that party, Hauser had so many apparent advantages. Montana's very first territorial legislature passed a series of special orders granting Hauser and his partners rights to form an array of businesses, including the Virginia City Gas Company, the Missoula Town Company, and the Gallatin Valley Ditch Company. Though these enterprises never came to fruition, they reflect the range of Hauser's geographic and business reach. He started the first national bank in Montana in his beloved hometown of Helena in March of 1866, and so he got the jump on capitalizing early businesses in the territory. His stature was such that he was appointed territorial governor for two years in the mid-80s (only possible during the Democratic administration of Grover Cleveland), traveling frequently to D.C. to advocate for Montana causes. He also served as a chief ally of the Northern Pacific Railroad in Montana, linking his fate to the original national railroad, given a massive land grant in 1864. Built on the path laid down by Isaac Stevens in his surveying work through the Northwest in 1855, NPRR seemed destined to transform Montana from a backwater to a major economic player in the 1870s. Yet the economic collapse of 1873 delayed construction, forcing the territory to wait until the early 1880s for the arrival of a dependable east-west conduit for materials in and products out. As an experienced railroad engineer from his youthful days in Missouri, Hauser saw opportunity in NPRR. He would take advantage of the railroad's extension into Montana by forming a series of syndicates to build branch lines to emerging communities such as Philipsburg and Red Lodge. In light of these many activities, one historian will describe Hauser as the most important economic force in Montana between 1870 and 1890. No wonder he will estimate his net worth at $1,955,000 and annual income at $337,000 in 1890.

Yet Hauser's hyperactivity may well account for his limited success. Business partners complain often about his lack of attention to detail, his lack of communication about how grand plans were unfolding, and his willingness to extend loans to family and friends with little or no collateral to assure repayment of the loans. He is frequently described as more of a convener than a manager of enterprises. His optimism—his refusal to see obstacles or potential failures—posed many a trap for his prospects.

Hauser also seems to have bet on the wrong horses in two important instances. His nearly religious mania about silver, the metal that succeeded gold as Montana's primary export and which would, for a brief time, serve as a foundation for the United States' monetary system, caused him to go all in with this metal in spite of the possibility the federal government could remove its support for silver. At this late date the passion for silver may seem quaint or inexplicable, yet a powerful third party, the Populists, based its platform in large part on the silver plank, and Hauser's own party, the Democrats, advocated fervently for silver coinage. Silver seemed to assure farmers and ranchers a fair price for their goods and the mine operators a market for their extractions. More to the point, by 1889, Montana produced one-fourth of the silver mined in the United States, and so it was indeed a lucrative metal. But in 1893, India's government will cease purchasing silver for coinage and the Sherman Silver Purchase Act will be repealed, ending the brief period of assured purchase of silver by the federal government and causing Hauser's overinvestment in that industry to prove catastrophic: "I will state to you that for the last eight or ten years I have been paying from eight to fourteen thousand dollars a year taxes. . . yet I could not today raise ten thousand on my entire property." Hauser's First National Bank, opened so early in Montana's territorial days, closes for six months, reopens, then will close for good in 1896. Richard Hugo could have been writing about Hauser in his extraordinary poem, "Degrees of Gray in Philipsburg": "The principal supporting business now / is rage. Hatred of the various grays / the mountain sends, hatred of the mill, / The Silver Bill repeal."

How different things might have turned out for Hauser. He sold his shares of the Hope Mine near Philipsburg in the 1880s, though he had helped found that very company with support from Missouri backers in the 1860s. Timing is all in mining as in life, and Hauser had surrendered an interest in a mine that might have softened the blow of silver's collapse. The Hope will continue to produce paying silver throughout the 1890s. Even more haunting, given his early arrival in Montana and his access to capital in the 1870s, Hauser might well have thrown in with the copper industry that transformed Daly and Clark into reigning plutocrats. At the very least he might have diversified his metal investments as a hedge against the failure of 1893.

Hauser's other prominent misjudgment? Backing the Northern Pacific Railroad instead of Hill's Great Northern and its key branch, the Montana Central Railroad. The Central, by connecting Butte, Great Falls, and the Great Northern's main route along the Hi-Line, assured high profits through the shipping of ore for smelting at Paris Gibson's new city near the Great Falls of the Missouri. Hauser's one-time friend and later competitor, Charles Broadwater, put his chips on Hill and so eclipsed his fellow Helenan before his untimely death.

Hauser's promotional efforts at Pony in July of 1889 illustrate his many strengths and weaknesses as a pioneering capitalist. Convinced that this region across the valley from Virginia City could prove a new gold bonanza, he and his partners will sink considerable capital into engineering reports and mining activities. Hauser also encourages the Northern Pacific to extend a branch line to the mines, no small expense, though one carried by the railroad company rather than Hauser. Yet in the end Hauser will report a personal loss of $30-40,000 on the scheme. In a seemingly rare moment of bitterness, he will speculate the mines may have been "salted," planted with gold to give the impression of great potential. Adding insult to injury, after Hauser and his partners withdraw from the venture, the mines will be reopened in 1900 and yield a substantial profit.

AUGUST

In which John Wesley Powell addresses the Constitutional Convention, the Ghost Dance comes to Fort Belknap, Deaf Bull leaves prison, Charles Broadwater opens his dream resort, and Nannie Alderson visits the Little Bighorn Battlefield.

The United States senate committee on irrigation held its first session at St. Paul Thursday, to hear delegations from South Dakota. The committee are now on their way to Glendive, where a meeting will be held Monday. The next session will be held at Miles City on the 6th, Billings on the 7th and Bozeman on the 8th, reaching Helena on the afternoon of the 9th, where they will be met by Senators Plumb and Jones, the latter now being a visitor in the National Park.

THE ONE-ARMED AUTODIDACT STANDS TO SPEAK TO Montana's Constitutional Convention, now approaching the end of its efforts to create the document that will form a state. By any measure, the speaker is a remarkable man, a living embodiment of nineteenth-century American ideals, an animated demonstration of the frontier virtues touted by Frederick Jackson Turner. John Wesley Powell is the son of British immigrants—ardent Methodists, hence John's middle name—who came of age in the upper Midwest when it was considered wilderness. He has a crackling mind that absorbs and synthesizes information at an almost overwhelming rate, so fast-paced that he struggles to put his ideas to paper. After managing his parents' Wisconsin farm during his adolescence, back-breaking work he will ever recall as formative and painful, he turned to teaching as the escape from that brutal labor. All the while he attended to the intellectual currents of his time, fixated by Lyell's geological theories and Darwin's revolutionary vision of evolution. Though raised in a devout Christian home, he is mesmerized by scientific theories that undermine many of that faith's assumptions.

Powell lost most of his right arm at the Battle of Shiloh, fighting on the Yankee side, but he never allows that disability to stop him. He led the first known expedition down the Colorado River in 1869, a feat so titanic it sealed his reputation and status for life. The Colorado was truly terra incognita, a blank space on the map of America, an unforgivable void in the national imagination. Powell summoned a motley crew of volunteers to steer wooden boats down one of the most challenging rivers in the world, providing, at last, a comprehensive survey of the mighty life source cutting through the Grand Canyon. That trip, with its heartache and strains, convinced Powell the West could never be viewed through eyes trained by lush eastern and Midwestern landscapes.

Though committed to the American mission to tame the wilderness, Powell believes with almost fanatic fervor the dominant paradigm of settlement is a catastrophe for settlers and land alike. The Northwest Ordinance of 1785 established the grid surveying system as the defining pattern for emerging territories. Land would be divided into townships, a square mile with six miles on each side. This basic unit could then be subdivided into sections of land claimed by individuals. The most common units of ownership would be 640, 320, and 160 acres. In many ways this approach implemented Enlightenment ideals of orderly, reasoned disposition of land. Yet if the system proved workable in the humid farmlands east of the Mississippi, it would, in Powell's view, be poorly adapted to the arid conditions west of the 100th meridian. Once settlers move into country receiving less than 20 inches of rain per year, the 160-acre homestead becomes a burden and a cross. Emigrants claiming land in the irrigated river valleys of the West need fewer than 160 acres to achieve good yields, while those on the dry plains need far more. In other words, the abstract, geometric system of sections imposed on the landscape will result in failed farms, failed communities, failed land. Powell had first propounded this view in his *Report on the Lands of the Arid Region of the United States* in 1878, a document so visionary that it still reads as radical in the twenty-first century.

With his sociable nature and quick mind, Powell ascends to lead the federal Bureau of Ethnology, dedicated to studying Indian tribes through collection of their languages, religious beliefs, and artifacts. This nineteenth-century overachiever will add the Geological Survey to his duties, insisting on a complete topographical survey of the United States to provide a realistic understanding of contour, climate, and settlement challenges throughout the United States, with special concern for the land beyond the Mississippi. One suspects those years on the farm baked into the man an unyielding realism about what it means to settle the continent.

Powell arrives in Helena in the company of senators conducting a listening tour of western territories and states, focused on questions of irrigation. These politicians have decidedly mixed views of Powell; at least one is flat-out skeptical about his outlandish theories of land use, for they would impose limits on determined capitalists' mastery of the land and its resources. Yet Powell will not be cowed or silenced when opportunity knocks to encourage a nascent state to adopt practical approaches to governing this beautiful but dry land. He presents himself as an "old pioneer," long familiar with the West, speaking to "tenderfeet," men who could learn a lesson or two from an experienced hand. Though the constitutional proceedings record applause in response to this odd appeal, listeners may have been offended by this patronizing attitude. Powell is laboring to establish his bona fides, his right to speak truth to delegates who could demonstrate the practical efficacy of his bold vision. He is also softening his auditors for a proposal both precise and revolutionary, creating counties based on drainage basins rather than the existing county lines, abstract, illogical, and inherited from territorial governance. The director of the Geographical Survey observes "in the western half of America, the local, the state, the territorial, county, governments and regulations and the national government are in no sense adapted to the physical conditions of the country."

Powell proffers, by contrast, a vision of Montana subdivided by what we would call an ecological sensibility:

> The whole area of Montana may be easily divided into drainage basin districts of country which constitute a geographical—a physical unity; a region like the Gallatin Valley, for example, with a river flowing down through the valley with its tributaries on either side, heading out from the mountains to the very rim of the Gallatin basin on either side. Every man who settles within the valley of Gallatin comes ultimately to be interested in every part of that valley, because it is the entire Gallatin valley, the whole drainage basin, gathers the water for his farm. . . . I think that each drainage basin in the arid land must ultimately become the practical unity of organization, and it would be wise if you could immediately adopt a county system which would be coincident with drainage basins, for in every such drainage basin you have got to have first the water courts. . . . [Y]ou have got to have local self government to manage that matter. Then the people who are interested in these waters are also interested in the timber, and the people who are interested in the waters

and agricultural lands are interested in the pasturage of those lands.

Given the constraints imposed by arid lands, citizens of the new state could cooperate to govern their land through attention to the conjoined needs of agriculture, mining, and logging. What a sharp rebuke to the thinking of men like Marcus Daly and A. B. Hammond, treating the commonwealth as their personal banking account, harvesting timber for the mines and railroads with thoughtless rapacity. What a rebuke to traditional politics played out in the contest between mining and agricultural interests, which often see their relationship as a zero-sum competition for resources and profit. Powell has perhaps unconsciously incorporated into his governing vision many of the values of his Methodist parents, imagining a society operating like a loving congregation, though one carefully constructed to account for conflict of interests (note the emphasis on courts centered in each drainage basin).

The Constitutional Convention follows precedent, however, establishing sixteen counties created haphazardly from the first territorial days down to the present moment, 1889. While those counties define regions, they in no way call for the kind of cooperative thinking and planning Powell preaches. The primary concern for delegates: determining the number of state senators and representatives each county will send to the legislature, numbers that define status and power. Powell's vision is simply too progressive, too radical for nineteenth-century citizens immersed in the ebb and flow of competing business interests. The "old pioneer" is asking for a paradigm shift, a recasting of entrenched attitudes toward land use, a rejection of the late-nineteenth-century capitalist ethos that is not just assumed but celebrated. Similar to Perry and Clara McAdow's plea for women's suffrage, Powell insists on changes to thinking and feeling that will come into vogue after bitter experience of limits and injustices imposed by conventional thought. Call it the dialectic of history, the testing and transforming of ideas over the course of generations. Such is the frustration and fascination of human time.

THE GHOST DANCE COMES TO THE FORT BELKNAP RESERVA-tion. A member of the Gros Ventre nation, visiting the Wind River Reservation in Wyoming, learns of the great awakening from Shoshone and Arapaho emissaries who have visited Wovo-ka, prophet and visionary, at Pyramid Lake in Nevada. The swift movement of what some would call the Messiah Craze is yet another sign of the frequent interchanges among Indian peoples in the troubled early reservation years.

Wovoka, son of a mystic Paiute, tells, "When the sun died [during an eclipse] . . . I went up to heaven and saw God and all the people who had died a long time ago. God told me to come back and tell my people they must be good and love one another, and not fight, or steal, or lie. He gave me this dance to give to my people." He further preaches that "by performing this dance at intervals, for five consecutive days each time, they would secure this happiness to themselves and hasten the event [of reunifi-cation with spirits of friends and relatives who had died]." As this original vision migrates through the plains north and south, it will take on new meanings, new implications. The Lakota at Pine Ridge, scene of the horrific Wounded Knee massacre in December of 1890, will interpret the dance as bringing about the return of the buffalo and the removal of the whites.

The Ghost Dance reaches Fort Belknap at a moment of cul-tural and spiritual demoralization, for the Aaniiih and Assini-boine have been confined to a small reservation in accord with the 1888 Sweetgrass Treaty. The bison are gone, the sacred cer-emonies are banned, and the ways to honor—acquiring wealth through horses, giving away to those in need, and war deeds—have evaporated. The people must depend upon annuities and half-hearted efforts at horse, cattle, and crop raising to fend off starvation. Yet the agent at Fort Belknap reports, "The past season has been a most discouraging one, owing to the general drought throughout Montana; consequently their crops are very poor. Their grain in most cases has been a failure, their yield being less than one-third of a fair average of successful years."

The people face an existential struggle to find meaning and purpose in this bleak linear world transplanted by the Americans. How to compensate for the vigor and beauty of the great animals—not just bison, but elk, deer, wolves, and bears—erased to make way for railroad, ranch, and mine? How to compensate for the pleasure and wisdom of movement in rhythm with the year, placing encampments where game, water, and warmth present themselves as gifts from the Maker? What is this static world, defined by boundaries, law, and clock time? Few Gros Ventre or Assiniboine adults are drawn to the Christian faith, taught at the boarding school nearby. Instead, the agent observes, "The old people are fast wedded to their ignorant prejudices, and practice rude, uncouth habits and customs, which interfere with the acquirement of civilized usages by the children and retards their advancement in education."

While the Ghost Dance proper will lose adherents on the Fort Belknap Reservation, an associated practice, the hand game, will continue into the 1890s. The hand game requires a team to use a spirit stick to guess which member of the opposing team is holding a bone button. The game recognizes the power of the spiritual world to guide the player in choosing the right hand, and in this way it extends and defends deep belief in the presence of spirit helpers well after reservation officials suppress "savage" rituals.

News of the Ghost Dance will also arrive at the Northern Cheyenne Reservation late in 1889, leading to an affecting scene as described by John Stands in Timber, a boy at the time:

This fasting was in connection with that Messiah Craze of 1890, and they claimed that they were doing it they receive visions of people who had been dead for a long time, even their relatives. Those priests came from the west, Ute Indians, or from the Shoshonis. . . . There were two Cheyennes came and two Sioux. I remember one Sioux's name was Short Bull, and the Cheyenne Porcupine, and White, and Magpie Eagle. No, not Magpie Eagle, but Magpie. They were the leaders starting the Messiah Craze dance here in 1890 and the government stopped it. There was a fort down here at the agency with a troop of soldiers, watching the Cheyennes all the time and keeping them inside the reservation, unless they had a permit to go to town or Crow Agency.

I remember when they started that dance, and afterwards I was told what kind of dance that they danced that day, between Birney and Ashland. We came along that way and saw a lot of people there down close to the river—a big ring of men holding each other, dancing around and around. Afterwards I learned it was the Messiah Craze dance. I was seven years old then. I didn't see just what they were doing, but there was a tepee there—they had a ceremony, and came out from the tepee and made that dance.

THE AGENT TO THE CROW RESERVATION REPORTS THAT ON August 20 Deaf Bull is released from prison in Minnesota. Deaf Bull had been a leader in Sword Bearer's rebellion the summer and fall of 1887. Heading a kind of proto-Ghost Dance movement, Sword Bearer presented himself as a prophet for his people, promising return to the old ways if they would follow him. Sword Bearer had a vision at a Cheyenne Sun Dance that he had

Deaf Bull, Fort Keogh, 1879. PHOTOGRAPH BY L.A. HUFFMAN. MONTANA
HISTORICAL SOCIETY RESEARCH CENTER PHOTOGRAPH ARCHIVES, HELENA,
MONTANA

been handed a great sword from the Creator, a sword that could cut down the white invaders and clear the ground for practicing the ceremonies and lifeways that sustained the Apsáalooke for hundreds of years. While he was resisted by such prominent leaders as Plenty Coups, he gathered to himself many younger men who were determined to reverse the erosion of ways toward honor, sacrifice, nation. As a dramatic demonstration of his beliefs, the visionary led twenty-four Crows on a horse raid among the Piegan in north-central Montana. That move violated all the fundamental principles of the reservation, dedicated to segregating the nations, confining them to defined property, inculcating "civilized" ways of farming and ranching, and above all breaking the traditions of raiding and horse-stealing that posed such an overt threat to the white settlers who feared for their livestock.

For three months following that horse raid, Sword Bearer evaded arrest or punishment, visiting other reservations and almost certainly journeying to the Big Horn Mountains to commune with his ancestors. That his ardor and conviction reached beyond the Crow Reservation became manifest when twenty Gros Ventre warriors from Fort Belknap attempted to join him in late October, a move halted by military and reservation officials.

On November 5, 1887, Sword Bearer's time ran out. He was shot down by one of his own tribesman, Fire Bear, a member of the tribal police, who blamed the visionary for stirring up discontent and violence on the reservation. Sword Bearer's rebellion did not die with him, however. Deaf Bull, an older chief with deep distrust of both the American agent and the Plenty Coups faction, led 150 warriors in continued resistance. But that act of defiance ended in chains and a journey to Fort Snelling in Minnesota.

The agent writing of Deaf Bull's release in 1889 claims "[h]e is greatly improved by his confinement; gives promises, which

Plenty Coups, head chief of the Crow Nation, 1906. Montana Historical Society Research Center Photograph Archives, Helena, MT

I consider sincere, of good conduct in the future, and I believe
that his influence will hereafter be wholly on the side of order,
obedience, and progress. He was much pleased to be once more
among his people." From the agent's point of view, Deaf Bull has
surrendered, capitulated, given himself over to the inevitable
movement of history. Yet it's equally possible he had adopted the
ways of Plenty Coups, whose youthful vision and mature actions
enabled "radical hope" in a people given every reason to despair
and surrender belief in their future. That which may appear victory for the invaders may, from another perspective, present as
a strategic choice to appear compliant while investing deeper
trust in the Apsáalooke. After all, Deaf Bull is "much pleased to
be once more among his people."

For in truth, Plenty Coups, while resistant to Sword Bearer's
militant stance, would use the visionary's death to advance
Crow interests. He would demand that the living leaders of
the uprising, including Deaf Bull, be spared imprisonment (a
futile demand, as it turned out). He would further insist that
the tribal police be disbanded or that individuals acceptable to
Plenty Coups and other emerging leaders such as Pretty Eagle
be appointed. This Apsáalooke leader seems to be thinking in
deep time and playing the long game. He is acting on his famous
vision, given to him through spiritual helpers when he was a
young man, and interpreted here by a tribal elder, Yellow Bear:

> "The dream of Plenty-coups means that the white men
> will take and hold this country and that their Spotted-
> buffalo will cover the plains. He was told to think for
> himself, to listen, to learn to avoid disaster by the experi-
> ences of others. He was advised to develop his body but
> not to forget his mind. The meaning of his dream is plain
> to me. I see its warning. The tribes who have fought the
> white man have all been beaten, wiped out. By listening as
> the Chickadee listens we may escape and keep our lands."

Plenty Coups imagines a future that will shelter and nourish his people. How could he navigate the contemporary reality of temporary Indian agents, confused federal authorities, nervous soldiers, and dispirited family and friends to achieve that future? He must choose among tangled, overlapping paths, seeing a way forward when no path seems open and sure. He must listen and learn, and pick his fights wisely. If his actions seem undramatic, tentative, compliant, he might reply that he is living out his vision, a powerful vision provided by great helpers, by observing, temporizing, and winning small victories that might add up to one great victory: The Apsáalooke will hold their land, even in the face of withering, persistent demands from the whites.

A Helena titan's dream becomes reality on August 26: The Broadwater Hotel and Natatorium opens west of Helena in the shadow of sheltering mountains. Charles Broadwater sees the elegant resort as a fitting jewel for his hometown and a destination for visitors from near and far drawn by the affluence and loveliness of Montana, a territory on the cusp of statehood and showing such promise in its mineral and agricultural wealth. The finely furnished Victorian hotel is, if anything, eclipsed by the mammoth natatorium, featuring "a lofty and picturesque structure of Moorish architecture, covering with its huge vaulted roof a bathing pool 300 feet long and 100 feet wide, at one end of which is a twin waterfall, pouring over great granite rocks, one cascade being of natural hot mineral water and the other of pure cold water."

Broadwater's career shows the power of personality to advance business interests. His path parallels, crosses, and diverges from Samuel Hauser's in many telling respects. Similar to Hauser, Broadwater left Missouri and landed early in what becomes Montana—in 1862, to be exact—and after initial forays into goldmining, he diverted his considerable energy and charm into freighting, taking the lead with the famous Diamond R freight-

The Broadwater Natatorium, 1890. Montana Historical Society Research Center Photograph Archives, Helena, Montana

ing company to move goods and wealth in and out of the territory. Broadwater formed an early friendship with Martin Maginnis, one of Montana's key political players during the territorial years, destined to serve as territorial delegate for twelve years and wield enormous influence on the destinies of Indian nations and railroads (he proved instrumental in radically reducing the Blackfeet Reserve north of the Missouri River in 1888, laying the ground for the Great Northern's expansion). Broadwater's next major business move put him into direct competition with Hauser and Granville Stuart: contracts to build and supply Fort Assinniboine and Fort Maginnis, located adjacent to the DHS Ranch in central Montana. Broadwater had sharp elbows as well as a winning personality, for he outmaneuvered his fellow Missourian for these lucrative contracts. Maginnis's friendship proved especially valuable in securing these agreements. Stuart's failure to grab the Fort Maginnis supply agreement proved one of the causes of his downfall as ranch superintendent.

The decisive break with Hauser arrived with the railroads. Broadwater befriended James J. Hill, the railroad tycoon from St. Paul, in the 1870s, a friendship that would bear fruit in a grand partnership that would fuse Montana to the upper Midwest. Broadwater turned to this alliance after Hauser prevented him from participating in the Northern Pacific's push into all parts of the growing territory. Along with Paris Gibson, Broadwater hosted Hill during a whirlwind tour of Montana in 1884, including stops at the Great Falls of the Missouri, Rimini goldmines west of Helena, and the wide open town of Butte. Hill later wrote Broadwater with his usual combination of vision and covetousness, "I cannot forget the many beautiful scenes of the few days spent with you in Montana, and I am more than ever impressed with the future of your territory. I do not recall another spot where I have ever seen so many natural advantages to build up a city as at Great Falls." Hill chose Broadwater to take the lead on surveying and building the Montana Central Railroad, a key artery leading from the mines of Butte to the smelters of Great Falls by way of Helena, there linking to Hill's Great Northern. The Montana Central completes its line to Butte in 1889. To compound his wealth and influence, Broadwater joins Hill and Paris Gibson in launching the Great Falls Water Power and Townsite Company, dedicated to building the new community near the dynamic falls on the Missouri River. These strategic alliances would not just create but sustain his wealth. He helps create the kind of vertically integrated business dreamed of by the likes of Marquis de Mores, but he has the backing of a railroad that controls freight rates, a key to financial gain for capitalists operating on the isolated northern tier.

In this way, Broadwater seems well positioned to survive the financial disruptions that will be caused by the 1893 Panic. He has not only seen the future of Montana's economy and helped bring it about, but he avoids retail politics that ensnare the likes of Daly, Clark, and Hauser. He prefers the backroom deal to the splashy public gesture. Broadwater is also notably skilled at organizing and completing schemes, a striking counterpoint to Hauser. Yet he will not live long enough to take advantage of his skill, charm, and luck. In 1892, he will die at the relatively young age of 52, less than three years after opening his fabled natatorium, a passing that will inspire bold headlines in Helena's *Independent*:

COL. BROADWATER DEAD.
Life Left His Weakened Body Without a Signal of Warning.
It Was a Grievous Shock to Helena Citizens of All Grades.
A Remarkable Man Whose Death is a Serious Loss
to City and State.
A Pioneer Who Was at One Time a Freighter
and Became a Millionaire.
He Was for Helena First and Worked Hard All the Time
for Her Prosperity.

The City is Mourning—Telegrams of Condolence From All
Sections of the Country.

As for Broadwater's hotel and natatorium, they will fall far
short of the builder's dream. The resort will be forced to close
just three years after his death, a victim in part of the financial
ups and downs of Gilded Age America. It will reopen sporadi-
cally in future years, but the buildings will be razed in 1946. Only
a few architectural remnants will recall a beautiful monument to
a man's wealth and a region's prospects. Charles Broadwater is a
Montana Ozymandias.

> IT WAS LATE SUMMER AND THE DAYS WERE BEAUTIFUL.
> No matter where we went on our drives, we would always
> wind up at the scene of Custer's last stand, above the Little
> Big Horn. There was a wonderful view up there, with the
> Big Horn mountains to the southwest and a long, low
> ridge to the west; and as we looked over the valley where
> the Sioux camp had been, we could almost see Custer's
> blue-coated troopers marching over the hills, on that ter-
> rible June morning. . . . [A]t the time I visited the scene,
> thirteen years after the battle, the bones had not been
> removed. The rains had washed them and the coyotes dis-
> turbed them.

A twenty-nine-year-old woman, sun-hardened by six years
in southeastern Montana, surveys the scene of a catastrophe for
at least three nations, the Lakota, Cheyenne, and United States.
Though viewing the spectacle from a buggy driven by a styl-
ish doctor, Nannie Alderson focuses on the memento mori, the
bones signifying death in the hot summer sun. Her memory
conjures the horror and trauma of that day, a turning point in
so many ways for all the peoples caught up in the vortex of violence.

Nanny T. Alderson, dressed for her 80th birthday party, 1940. MONTANA HISTORICAL SOCIETY RESEARCH CENTER PHOTOGRAPH ARCHIVES, HELENA, MONTANA

Custer's battlefield, circa 1895. The white posts mark where soldiers' bodies were found. MONTANA HISTORICAL SOCIETY RESEARCH CENTER PHOTOGRAPH ARCHIVES, HELENA, MONTANA

Alderson lives out the legacy of that cataclysm. A diehard Southerner (her father was killed early in the Civil War fighting on the Confederate side), Nannie fell hard for a dashing cowboy, Walt Alderson, during a visit to her aunt in Kansas. Swept up in the cattle fever of the early 1880s, Nannie and Walt claimed land on Rosebud Creek in 1883, occupying terrain seized from the victors on that June day in 1876. They were convinced a small investment would yield a vast profit. They experienced the cross-currents of competing desires on this contested ground, enacting the American search for wealth and status, interacting repeatedly with restless Cheyenne, Lakota, and Crow, and withal struggling to make a go in a land that takes as much as it gives. No wonder Alderson will write with understated irony, "When you live so close to the bare bones of reality, there is very little room for sentiment."

Despite this disavowal of sentiment, Nannie relates with a mixture of pride and nostalgia the building of their first ranch on Rosebud Creek. The writer invests charm and emotion in that wilderness home, a fascinating counterpoint to the disillusioning ranch home described in B. M. Bower's *Lonesome Land*. Nannie is, after all, a young bride, a Ruth in alien corn, or rather sage and pine, far from lush, cultivated West Virginia. In this touching, at times harrowing memoir she will compose in old age, Nannie never forgets how young and full of energy they all were. She must depend upon the kindness of cowboys, a surprisingly domestic, helpful bunch, if prone to occasional acts of folly. She cannily describes their mixed reputation and subsequent transformation into knights of the plains: "Few families living in Montana had their cowboys live with them as we did. Nobody then thought of them as romantic. They were regarded as a wild and undesirable lot of citizens, but I always thought there was much injustice in this. Nice people in Miles City would as soon have thought of inviting a rattlesnake into their homes as a cowboy."

The Aldersons were unintentional participants in one of the central dramas of Indian-white conflict in the region, their loss a major prop for ranchers' request in May 1889 that the Northern Cheyenne Reservation be abolished. A silly prank by a thoughtless cowboy burned down the house. Since the 1884 incident between Hal Taliaferro, cowboy, and Black Wolf, Cheyenne chief, disclosed conflicting worlds, conflicting understandings, it is best told in two voices, first Nannie Alderson's, then John Stands in Timber's. Nannie and Walt did not witness the events described, for they were in Miles City as Nannie delivered their first child, and so Alderson's account is based on Hal's recollections:

> An Indian sub-chief named Black Wolf . . . had brought
> his lodge to visit on the Rosebud not far from our ranch.
> On a day of melting snow, he had come round begging
> for food and tobacco; the boys fed him, and afterwards
> he sat down to smoke on a pile of fence posts, some yards
> from our door. . . . When Hal looked out the door and
> saw the Indian sunning himself, he said to Reinhart:
>
> "I'll bet you five dollars I can put a hole through that old
> Indian's hat without touching his head."
>
> The other man of course replied: "I'll bet you can't."
>
> Hal drew his six shooter and fired, just nicking the In
> dian's scalp. Black Wolf of course was furious; he could
> not and would not believe that Hal had not meant to kill
> him. . . . [T]he Indians, the whole lodge, were in posses
> sion. Squaws and papooses were seated in a semi-circle in
> the front yard, while the bucks were carrying out bureau
> drawers and emptying the contents in the midst of them.
> . . . Hal, realizing that they meant to set fire to it, rode up
> to them as near as he dared, promising them beef, coffee,

Black Wolf, 1901. Montana Historical Society Research Center Photograph Archives, Helena, Montana

ponies, and tobacco. But when they started shooting at him, tearing up the earth under his horse, he realized it was no use, and the men could do nothing but ride up on top of a hill and watch while the house roared into flames.

[CHIEF BLACK WOLF] MUST HAVE COME TO THAT RANCH about noon and stopped in there. . . . According to his own story, one of them came out with a plate full of stuff to eat, he . . . went down on the grass and . . .started eating. . . . the way I was told, these cowboys came out . . . and one of them took out a six-shooter and told the others, "I bet I can knock off his hat without hitting him.". . . [H]e pointed at his head, and he did pull the trigger, and he did shoot too low. And the Indian dropped.

. . . . Black Wolf when he did come out of it was lying on his back. . . . He got up all right and, just about the time he started walking away, he said the earth began to turn and he fell over. . . . So he crawled on this knees and hands. . . . Once in a while he would try to get up and walk, and he could not make it. . . .

So he . . . just crawled, and he must have crawled about little more than a mile before somebody met him and picked him up and made a report down to the village. . . . And they sent somebody up the road to notify all the other men, and all the men came down and organized a war party. When they came up close to attack on that ranch, and went in and shot into the windows here and there, and broke in and robbed the house and took whatever they wanted, and then set it afire and burned the ranch down. . . .

The stories' differences reveal far more than their similarities. While Alderson emphasizes that Black Wolf was accompanied

by his family, Stands in Timber highlights the chief's single-
ness, his isolation, his lack of threat. While Alderson dismisses
the wound as "nicking the scalp," Stands in Timber tells of a
harrowing effort by a seriously wounded man to return to his
people. While Alderson insinuates Black Wolf led the attack on
the ranch, Stands in Timber makes it clear others formed a war
party to avenge an act of violence and insult. Underlying these
counter-tales are years of incomprehension, distrust, and fear, as
shown through such objectifying language as "begging for food
and tobacco" and "these cowboys."

American law intervened in the conflict, seeking to appre-
hend Hal but unable to do so when he fled the region. Authorities arrested thirteen Cheyenne for destruction of property, and
four were convicted and sent to the territorial penitentiary. Yet
Alderson's bitterness was not assuaged by formal legal proceedings. She and Walt risked so much to build that first home, and
she lost many items valued for their connection to her Southern
family. As she observed, such losses recur each time the owner
seeks them for special occasions or to inspire memory.

Yet Alderson's relationship with her Cheyenne neighbors
proved far more complicated than a simple tale of violence, loss,
and grievance. Nannie tells in affecting detail of her enduring
friendship with Little Wolf, the very chief who led his people on
a heroic journey from Indian Territory to the Tongue River in
1878. Alderson met a humbled, lonely Little Wolf, since he had
been ostracized by his nation after he killed a fellow Cheyenne
in his role as tribal policeman. (In this sense Little Wolf's story
mirrors Fire Bear's, the Crow tribal policeman who killed Sword
Bearer.) If at first blush such a relationship between emigrant
and Indian seems unlikely, even incredible, careful reading of
Alderson's memoir yields a clue to their bond: both felt displaced, separated from homeland and family, alone, and longing
for connection. It might not be too far a stretch to suggest they
developed a father-daughter relationship, since Little Wolf was
especially keen to spend time with Nannie and her children, as

though he had adopted (or been adopted into) a new family. To her credit, Alderson will not overstate her understanding of this friendship. She will admit to lingering uncertainty, even confusion about what drew together these two people, raised in vastly different worlds.

Despite those differences, Little Wolf will serve as the most moving witness to the event that changed Nannie's life forever, the passing of the cowboy who had courted her in Kansas and dreamed big of cattle ranching in Montana: "The papooses [her children] did not get sick in Miles City, but my husband was killed there, and they said that when Little Wolf heard about it he cried like a child. He would come to our old ranch and follow the people around, asking everyone to tell him about it, although of course he did not know English very well—and they said he never seemed satisfied until he understood how the accident had happened." Nannie and Walt had abandoned the ranch life to raise their children in the most prominent town in the region. There, Walt will take up horse raising and wrangling, since the price of horses rises dramatically in the 1890s. Once again, however, larger economic processes will not favor his choice: the 1893 financial panic and economic downturn that fell Sam Hauser will depress the market for horses. In an ironic twist, one of those animals will prove Walt's undoing: A bucking horse kills him during feeding time.

". . . [A]fter my husband's death, I was no longer a bride who went west, nor a woman who was helping to open up a new country; I was merely an overworked mother of four, trying to make ends meet under conditions which were none too easy." But Nannie Alderson proves a sticker—she will help her daughter operate a dude ranch near Sheridan, Wyoming, for many years, before taking the time to narrate her story to Helena Huntington Smith. This daughter of the South will prove up as one of the most telling witnesses to that time of hope and dread, Montana in the 1880s and 90s.

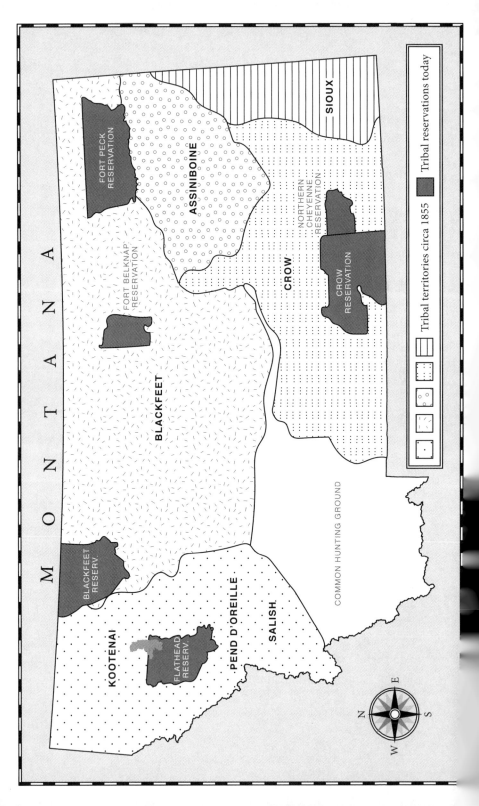

SEPTEMBER

In which the Fort Peck agent accounts for the Assiniboine and Sioux, Rose Gordon starts school in White Sulphur Springs, Mad Wolf praises George Bird Grinnell, the Great Northern Railway is born, and F. Augustus Heinze arrives in Butte.

———

For some time past it has been given out in Democratic circles that the torchlight procession of last evening would be a revelation to spectators. . . . At the appointed hour the line of march was formed and as it wended over and through the central portion of the city it seemed interminable. The procession was composed of nearly two thousand men representing the following organizations: Headed by the Emmet Guard band, there followed the Silver Bow Tammany club, the Silver Bow County Democracy, the Parrot Democratic club, the South Butte Democratic club, the Scandinavian Democratic club and a large contingent of the bone and sinew of the camp. . . . It took exactly thirty-five minutes for the procession to pass the corner of Main and Park streets.

———

THE RETIRING INDIAN AGENT AT FORT PECK ISSUES HIS report for 1889 on September 2. D. O. Cowen provides a cold accounting of conditions on the reservation, created the year before by the Sweetgrass Treaty with the eastern boundary at Big Muddy Creek, the western boundary the mouth of the Milk River, the southern boundary the Missouri River, and the upper boundary 40 miles north of the Missouri. The most helpful aspect of the treaty establishing these reservation boundaries: guarantee of $165,000 in annuities for ten years at a time of severe drought, exterminated bison, and decimated wildlife. Cowen's bureaucratic approach may reflect the impatience of a man ready to leave his post, but it also typifies the statistical analysis of Indian lives dominant in the Department of Interior and the ethnographic profession emerging at this very moment in American culture.

In this sense, the agent's methods align with those of John Wesley Powell, director of the federal Bureau of Ethnology. Powell's interest in anthropology is of a piece with his advocacy for government units based on drainage basins—the aboriginals must be converted to American citizens to pave the way for a new, innovative form of governance in the arid West. Powell adheres to the most influential theory of cultures from the late-nineteenth century, that of Lewis Henry Morgan. Morgan argues for a stage theory of human development leading from savagery (hunting and gathering) to barbarism (early agriculture) to civilization (contemporary Europe and the United States). To his credit, Morgan does not see this hierarchy as justifying eradicating Indian peoples or viewing them as different in kind from whites. Those caveats cannot conceal the implication, the assertion that native nations must be converted to civilized society, an underpinning of the late-nineteenth century federal Indian policy.

Writing within this emerging sociological regime, Cowen notes a total of 1,702 Yankton Sioux and Assiniboine Indians live on the reservation, though he adds, alarmingly, that as many as 300 members of the tribes were not accounted for at the time of the census. He helpfully, if condescendingly, adds that of the total, "91 are mixed blood; 610 wear citizens' dress wholly and 218 wear citizens' clothing in part, and there are 296 of school age."

Under the heading "Civilization," Cowen asserts reservation occupants "built and occupied 160 log cabins the past year. The total number of dwellings occupied is 480." (The agent may not realize that many cabins are infested with bed bugs and so reservation occupants still prefer to sleep in tipis during the warmer months.) However, the agent is sad to note "[t]here has been no advance morally by these Indians outside those in attendance at school." And indeed, the boarding school is clearly a point of pride for Cowen, since a new building is under construction, and the current facility accommodates 165 pupils. Those pupils are fortunate enough to benefit from a full set of opportunities and a diverse curriculum: "At this school in the recitation rooms are taught object lessons, orthography, geography, reading, writing, and arithmetic, and one hour each evening devoted to singing and varied exercises, interesting and instructive. The industries taught are farming and raising truck, the use of implements and tools, butter-making, dress-making and sewing generally, cooking, baking, and kitchen and dining-room details, washing and ironing, care of stock, cutting wood, etc." There is little effort to point students toward professional lives—presumably they have a long hill to climb to reach the lower levels of civilized life, and so the higher occupations must remain out of reach for the time being.

Miscellaneous observations include mention that no allotments have been made due to "the Indians not being sufficiently advanced to take lands in severalty." Encouragingly, however, "[t]he Indians cut 1,600 cords of wood—600 cords for agency and school. The rest was sold to steam-boats plying on the Missouri River, traders, and military contractors." And perhaps most hopeful from the agent's point of view, clearly conforming to the Commissioner of Indian Affairs' stated goal of converting the natives to civilized property owners, "There are owned by Indians 560 horses, 461 cattle, including cows, calves, and oxen; 300 sheep and 700 domestic fowls." These numbers are so precise that a skeptical reader might wonder whether Agent Cowen could be inventing convenient statistics. A more likely explanation for this precision, however, is that the agent takes seriously the job of enumerating and itemizing Sioux and Assiniboine progress as measured on the scale of American culture. These numbers matter, for they provide the bureaucrat's means to gauge a people's advance from savagery to civilization.

AN AFRICAN AMERICAN CHILD STARTS SCHOOL IN HER beloved hometown of White Sulphur Springs: "It gives me great pleasure to tell you about the days I went to school. We did not have knindergarten [kindergarten], in White Sulphur Springs, at the time. So, I was six-years-old, when mama took me to school." Born in 1883 to an ex-slave mother and black immigrant from Scotland, Rose Gordon would become a leading citizen of this central Montana community, a source of historical memory, healing balm, and uncommon decency.

Education would always be one of Rose's core convictions and desires. She will remember fondly her elementary years dedicated to "ABC, drawing, playing with blocks, and singing childern songs." Her middle and high school years will summon memories of "Shakespeare and all the great poets from which we learned many things that helped us through life." Rose will become her class's valedictorian, a moving honor: "The place was filled to see the class of 1904 get their diplomas. My oration, was about the progress of the colored race, in these United States of America." That speech will conclude with praise for Booker T. Washington and his vision for racial uplift, values Rose seems to absorb into her intellectual bloodstream, for she will live out many of Washington's beliefs. Following high school, she will attend nursing school for a short time in Helena, but her beloved mother, widowed by her husband's death in a railroad accident, will need financial and emotional support, and so Rose will return to work as a house maid and hotel clerk. She will not surrender her commitment to education, however, for she will seek advanced training throughout her adulthood, including certifi-

Taylor Gordon and his sister, Rose B. Gordon, 1960, White Sulphur Springs, Montana. Montana Historical Society Research Center Photograph Archives, Helena, Montana

cation as a massage therapist. She will put this training to use as she treats a wide range of ailments in that tough ranching, logging, and mining country. Rose is never more Montanan than in her taking on a variety of jobs throughout her life to make ends meet, including managing a restaurant and running (unsuccessfully) for mayor of White Sulphur Springs.

These diverse roles seem to provide insight into the lives of community members, for Rose will prove herself an exceptionally observant citizen of her home region. In the local newspaper, she will publish many articles about the people of White Sulphur Springs and the surrounding ranches and towns. None is more moving than her memoir of her mother's migration to Montana, leading with the unforgettable title, "My Mother Was a Slave." And her recollection of an infamous woman's stopover will stand beside any description of that controversial westerner:

> I must tell you about the thrill we children had the day they told us that Calamity Jane was coming in on the six-horse stage coach. She was a legend to us. The day came and we saw her. She was a rugged looking woman and weather beaten. When she smiled at us you could see so much kindness in her face. She wore dark clothes and a black cap that came down to her neck. It was very cold. We went to bed that night very happy. We had the pleasure of seeing "Calamity Jane."

This gifted memoirist and citizen is also older sister to one of the startling talents out of Montana history, Taylor Gordon, who will become a leading performer of Negro spirituals during the Harlem Renaissance. While Taylor has received much notoriety in Montana culture, including serving as the inspiration for Ivan Doig's *Prairie Nocturne*, Rose has receded from view. Yet hers is an equally affecting story of service, memory, and grace. Her description of Calamity Jane's smiling face would seem an apt summary of her own character and appeal. Certainly this letter to a white woman who has treated her shabbily speaks of a human being both profoundly aware of prejudice and determined to overcome it with charity:

> I have just heard the latest gossip that Mrs. Winters is being asked to resign from her lodge for keeping me company.
>
> Mrs. Ashford can you prove that my company is such that one would be damaged by my association?
>
> I know my skin is black [which] I can't help, you might have been born black would that necessarily have to corrupt your character?
>
> Mrs. Ashford I pity you as a mother would pity a child, and each night as you pray ask God to teach you to understand that each race is [his] own and that you are not to abuse and wound their feelings.

A VISIT BETWEEN TWO MEN OF STATUS, EACH DISTINGUISHED by knowledge and notable deeds, yields a statement of gratitude: "You are good. . . . You stopped the lies here, rubbed them out and all the crooked work before. It was bad. . . . If it hadn't been for you it would still have been 'Tomorrow, Tomorrow.' If not for you we get nothing."

So says Mad Wolf, Piegan chief and keeper of the Beaver Bundle, to George Bird Grinnell, publisher of *Field and Stream* and lover of the West. These words are spoken during a council meeting among tribal leaders at a moment of deep crisis. Just a year earlier—on May 1, 1888—the U.S. Senate had ratified the Sweetgrass Treaty, reducing the Indians' vast reservation, encompassing all of the land between the Missouri River and the Canadian border, to three much smaller parcels at Fort Peck,

George Bird Grinnell on Grinnell Glacier. MONTANA HISTORICAL SOCI-
ETY RESEARCH CENTER PHOTOGRAPH ARCHIVES, HELENA, MONTANA

Blackfoot man on horse with travois, Glacier National Park, circa 1910-1914.
Minnesota Historical Society

Fort Belknap, and Browning, reserved for the Assiniboine and Nakoda, Gros Ventre (Aaniiih) and Assiniboine, and Piegan Blackfeet, respectively. In truth, the United States government coerced the agreement, recognizing the affected nations' need for annuities following the extermination of the buffalo, the threat of starvation, and the ever-present danger of disease and malaise. In the words of the Blackfeet nation's tribal history,

> The Blackfeet people, now confined to the reservation borders, were to have psychological, physical, social, spiritual, and economic changes that would place their cultural lifestyles in chaos by disturbing the usual patterns of activities and behaviors. The winter camp tradition, away from the extreme mountain cold, was no longer possible without retribution of the most severe punishments. The complete functioning of Blackfeet survival which required a larger area of resources had shrunk from the headwaters of the Yellowstone River north to the Birch Creek.

As the tribal history suggests, the Piegans' loss of land is far more extensive than that formalized in the Sweetgrass Treaty. The 1855 Lame Bull Treaty, negotiated between Isaac Stevens and the confederated Blackfeet nations and the Aaniiih, set aside the region between the Missouri and Yellowstone rivers as a Common Hunting Area for all nations. That land had simply been taken by white settlers such as James Fergus and Granville Stuart without a thought for compensation. One of Mad Wolf's goals before his death in 1902 will be to seek redress for this theft.

Why, then, does the Piegan leader speak those words to Grinnell at this time of crisis? Grinnell had published a scathing editorial in the *New York Times* on March 4, 1889, calling out the notoriously corrupt Indian agent, Mark Baldwin. Grinnell's words reveal the conscience, the values, the historical vision of a leading liberal of his time, a friend of Theodore Roosevelt's who demonstrates far more respect for indigenous peoples' humanity than the New York politician and sometime rancher, yet holds to the ideal of assimilation. Premising that "I am not an Eastern sentimentalist," that is, not one of those friends of the Indian often satirized by Westerners, Grinnell asserts the Piegan "are now being treated in a way that ought to make every American ashamed. . . ." Observing that the nation had been reduced to 1,500 by hunger and disease, especially following the horrific Starvation Winter of 1884, in which 600 members of the nation died due to government neglect, Grinnell offers that the Piegan understand they must make the transition to an agricultural life in ten years or face further starvation. Unfortunately, Agent Baldwin has done everything in his power to deny them the means and opportunity to fulfill that promise. Instead, "[t]his agent is a man who cares nothing for the condition of the people under his charge, and is using his office solely for his own selfish ends." The editorialist then catalogs the agent's failures, including misappropriating government property and allowing ranchers to graze as many as 20,000 head of cattle on Piegan land. No wonder "[t]he Indians bitterly resent this second invasion." Baldwin earns his dubious nickname through his delaying tactics, for "[t]he Piegans call their agent 'Tomorrow' from his habit of saying when they ask anything of him, 'Yes, yes, to-morrow.' But with him to-morrow never comes."

While Grinnell's appeals are compelling, impressive and effective (Baldwin is in fact removed as agent), they lead to a conclusion that may read as chilling in our own time. What is Baldwin's ultimate ethical lapse? "The agent's failure to acquaint the Indians with their rights to land in severalty is a substantial offense. Congress has provided that the Indians should be instructed in the ways of civilization, and the Dawes bill was passed in order to give each Indian a chance to possess a bit of land of his own, over which he might exercise just such rights as a white man has over his real estate." Grinnell refers to the 1887 act of Congress, named for a leading Republican senator from Massachusetts, that seemed destined to extinguish Indian title to reservation lands by converting indigenous people to individuals holding their pieces of property like proper American citizens. Though designed with fervent idealism—Dawes, so committed a Republican he served as one of the pallbearers at Lincoln's funeral, was a persistent believer in the federal government's role as protector of minority rights—the Severalty Act becomes a brilliant machine to dispossess Indians of land guaranteed under treaties between sovereign nations. If the bill's sponsors assumed severalty would lead to civilizing savages, other, more materialistic individuals would recognize an opportunity to scoop up land parceled out in 160 units and available for the taking once recognized tribal members had claimed their allotments.

Given Grinnell's commitment to allotment, Mad Wolf's earnest thanks may seem naïve or misguided. Such a conclusion underestimates the Piegan leader's political and cultural acuity. Grinnell has been effective at removing an immediate and awful barrier to tribal members' well-being, and so he may be able to realize larger goals for a nation seeking justice in a brutal environment that combines well-intentioned assimilationists, determined railroad tycoons, economic boosters, greedy agents, and indifferent politicians. In the end, despite his sincere belief in native peoples' rights, Grinnell will help secure the "Backbone of the World," the Piegans' sacred mountains, for Glacier National Park. While the Blackfeet initially retain their rights to hunt, fish, and follow their spiritual practices in the "Ceded Strip," those rights will be denied once the national park is established in 1910. The determined conservationist will believe he has saved spectacular country from exploitation by acquisitive Americans, yet his Piegan friends will see his actions as a betrayal.

Mad Wolf, Piegan chief. MONTANA STATE UNIVERSITY LIBRARY

Perhaps that's why Mad Wolf will turn to Walter McClintock, who first arrives on the Blackfeet Reservation in 1896 as part of a forest survey team and develops a close, abiding friendship with the keeper of the Beaver Bundle. Mad Wolf will adopt McClintock as a member of the Piegan nation, a solemn honor that intimates the leader's desire to secure more advocates for Piegan rights. If anything, McClintock will prove more feckless than Grinnell, frequently overpromising political influence to gain access to his hosts' lodges and stories. Yet no less a Piegan historian than Darrell Robes Kipp will acknowledge McClintock's value to contemporary Blackfeet, for he will preserve so much cultural knowledge in his books *The Old North Trail* and *Old Indian Trails*. If this young man in search of a new home in the West, so typical of wanderers such as Grinnell and Frank Linderman, seems duplicitous in his political promises, he will deliver on another promise, serving as witness and recorder at a moment of deep cultural trauma who passes along vital teachings, memory, possibility. He also offers a moving portrait of his teacher and adopted father:

> One afternoon in midsummer, while riding with Siksikakoan across the plains, we met Mad Wolf near Willow Creek. He was alone and signified his desire to speak with me. He was standing with his blanket drawn closely around him. His long hair tinged with gray fell loosely over his shoulders. From his neck hung a medicine whistle made from the wing-bone of an eagle. In his back hair, a single eagle feather stood erect. When I had dismounted, he warmly shook my hand. For a moment, he gazed into my face with eyes as penetrating as those of an eagle. Then, with head erect, he addressed me in a strong and earnest voice: "I have never taken a son from among the white men, but I now wish to adopt you as my son . . . . I am growing old, and it is probable that I will go before

you to dwell with the Great Spirit, for you are still a young man. When I am gone you will then be left to help and to advise my people."

THE GREAT NORTHERN RAILWAY IS BORN ON SEPTEMBER 16, 1889. The Blackfeet Reserve was killed so James Jerome Hill's railroad could live.

Canadian by birth, American by business practices, and global by vision, Hill can be taken as the very avatar of the acquisitive capitalist of the nineteenth century. He emigrated from Ontario to St. Paul in the 1850s, then worked as a clerk, trader, and shipper for years in the city at the headwaters of the Mississippi. His early years in Minnesota proved a perfect training ground for negotiating shipping rates, anticipating costs, and acquiring goods at favorable prices. He acquired a steamship company that worked the Red River Valley extending from St. Paul to Winnipeg, building his first fortune in the country made famous by Louis Riel. In his maturity, he acquired the St. Paul, Minneapolis, and Manitoba Railroad (usually shortened to the Manitoba) that served as precursor for the Great Northern. He carefully, if frenetically, built the Manitoba as a regional transportation power, covering Minnesota, eastern North Dakota, and southern Manitoba. Then he cast his eyes westward. He could feel the economy, the future of the North American continent tilting east-west rather than north-south following the Civil War. He dreamed of a transcontinental railroad that would link the Pacific to the upper Midwest. He was caught up in that very old vision of the Passage to India, the almost tangible sense that European culture could be carried to the Orient via America. Underpinning this vision was the racialist belief in the superiority of the Anglo Saxon "people," presumed to be advanced in intellect, energy, and morality. The railroads, along with machines such as the telegraph and steamships, provided

James J. Hill, circa 1865. MINNESOTA HISTORICAL SOCIETY

the technology to actualize that vision. No wonder Hill adopted the middle name of Jerome, the same as Napoleon Bonaparte's brother, a nominal and emotional connection to the greatest man of the railroad baron's century.

But to realize that vision, Hill would need to claim land held by Indians. He went to work lobbying with full force for the reduction of the Blackfeet Reserve in 1886 and 1887, joining the likes of Martin Maginnis and Henry Dawes (yes, Dawes of the Severalty Act) in compelling federal permission to dispossess the Indians of 17,500,000 acres. Though President Grover Cleveland put up surprising initial resistance to Hill's efforts, ultimately, inevitably, typically, the U. S. government negotiated terms with the affected tribal nations in February, 1887, and the Napoleon of the West could launch an extraordinary building project: extend his railroad from Minot to Helena in a single building season. The line would follow the Northern Overland Route—the Minnesota-Montana Road—first blazed by James Fisk and early settlers such as Nathaniel Langford and James Fergus in 1862 as gold attracted emigrants to a notoriously isolated region. Denied the Yellowstone corridor by the inefficient but persistent Northern Pacific Railroad, Hill adopted the Milk River as his lifeline. Even accounting for the unusually level and tractable land to be crossed, this was an extraordinary achievement. Hill drove himself to utter collapse making it happen, guiding the construction work onsite. This titanic effort only made sense by accounting for the development of Great Falls as a smelting center for ore extracted in Butte, with vital coal available in extensive mines east of the new city on the Missouri River. As was typical of railroad tycoons of the period (think Frederick Billings on the Yellowstone River), the St. Paul railroader invested in businesses and townsites in Great Falls to increase his payoff.

In these ways the capitalist could hedge his bets on a risky venture, for whatever the epic grandeur of his transcontinental and transoceanic vision, he would need to figure out how to pay the fixed costs of a railroad vastly overextended. Think of all those miles of track running through virtually depopulated land—how would it pay to ship materials to the hinterland if there was little to supply or few goods to transport east? Following the silver collapse of 1893, Hill will set his eyes on fixing this intractable problem: inspire and market the homestead boom that would have desperate consequences for human beings and region, including the bust of the 1910s and '20s and the massive dust storms of the '30s. In the words of Joseph Kinsey Howard, a great Montana writer and historian,

> Thus was the stage set for Jim Hill, tough man who loved a tough land. There was in him something of the bravura of northwestern plainsmen who had been known to walk deliberately and unnecessarily into a blizzard or into murderous hail, mocking the gods of storm, testing their own stamina. Jim Hill would show the scoffers back east. He would force this "wasted" empire into the frame of his vision: his pretty picture of little green fields and little white houses and big red barns, with lightning rods to deflect the shafts of the northwest's primeval gods.

All that lay in the future, however. In 1889, transfixed by a vision and feeling flush with the completion of the Montana Central Railroad joining Butte mines to Great Falls smelters, Hill reorganizes the Manitoba as the Great Northern Railway, attracting massive international investment to complete the railroad's push to the Pacific. In his usual canny way, he builds a financial underpinning that will survive even the terrible crash of 1893, and so the Great Northern will be the only railroad serving Montana to evade receivership. And he accomplishes this titanic feat without the benefit of the massive land grant provided the Northern Pacific. Hill takes as the railroad's symbol the mountain goat, inspired by the gift of a stuffed goat from none other than "Broad," Charles Broadwater, his main man in

Montana. In order to link the ocean to the prairies, he needs to settle the haunting question of how to cross the imposing Rocky Mountains (the Blackfeets' "Backbone of the World"). Can he locate a pass at an easy grade to reduce costs of construction and hauling? December will provide the answer—and heartbreak for Paris Gibson, Great Falls' founder and unstinting promoter. James Jerome Hill seems to have had a peculiar talent for breaking hearts.

Could you spot a financial and mining genius, one willing to shave his ethics as close as his fine cheek, when he arrives on a September day in Butte, carrying his elite upbringing, advanced education, and sheer bravado? Would you know him for the refined rascal he will prove to be, or would he seem the very figure of insouciance, a kind of relaxed, lazy elegance, a man's man, to be sure, but hardly to be feared? How could you know he would turn out to be one of the big players, contesting ownership and status with Daly and Clark? He would, in the end, founder, not just on the rocks of that competition, but on the rocks of his own compulsions. Yet, for a time, he would stir things up, shake the power structure in one of the world's most important mining towns, and even threaten the financial well-being of the nation's most powerful company. F. Augustus Heinze, "Fritz," would take Montana and the world on quite a ride.

Born into an elite merchant family of German origin in New York, Fritz received a world-class education, almost in spite of his lackadaisical attitude toward academic routine. His father's patriarchal insistence on rigorous training in Germany, followed by a mine engineering education at Columbia University, prepared the young man well for the inside games he would come to play on the richest hill on earth. Glancing back at his youth from the perspective of the entire life's arc, an observer can detect Fritz's strategy: invest only as much energy as required to

F. Augustus Heinze. Montana Historical Society Research Center Photograph Archives, Helena, Montana

master the academic details while gathering social and financial capital, learning the fine art of seducing men and women, and anticipating opportunity before anyone could know what hit them.

Heinze begins his elaborate Butte campaign by taking a modest engineer's job with the Boston and Montana Company. Though to call Heinze's efforts a campaign seems to overstate his advance planning—surely improvisation will play its part, for the young man is a kind of jazz master in the barroom known as Butte. He may well have been simply curious, uncertain what he would find in this epicenter of the American mining industry, gauging opportunity and competition. What a clever, nondescript perch from which to study the playing field. As with his formal academic training, Heinze will not waste too much energy on his formal responsibilities. Instead, he will conform to his role while analyzing intently, deeply the workings of the Butte copper industry, from extraction to smelting to refining. Observing Daly and Clark, as well as lesser magnates such as James Murray, he realizes a true copper titan must control the smelting process to maximize profits, an understanding he will later put to use. During his time at the Boston and Montana he will also come to know the vein structure of that famous hill as well as any human being. This knowledge will prove especially lucrative when he makes his big move in the early 1890s, for he will exploit an esoteric mine law to rob the Boston and Montana blind.

After resigning from the Boston and Montana and establishing his own company, the Montana Ore Purchasing Company, Heinze will return to his hometown to secure financing for the plan that has fully formed in his clever head. His timing is unfortunate, however, for the Panic of 1893 will stall capital investment, especially in risky mining ventures, and so he must work for a time at a mining journal in New York, biding his time, as it were, allowing capital to find him. This quality of waiting, of making oneself available, of being open to opportunity but none too pushy, also separates young Heinze from his seasoned and impatient seniors in the Butte mining wars. And it finds him capital in the form of the Lewisohn brothers, among the wealthiest of the great financiers of the Gilded Age. Armed with their backing, his plan, and his sheer bravado, Heinze will return to Butte, though it must be added, he will not return alone. His brothers Arthur and Otto literally and figuratively join him, forming a critical alliance of mining engineer, lawyer, and banker. If it's tempting to imagine Fritz's victory as a lone man's triumph over antagonistic forces, one would do well to remember the sage counsel and much-needed camaraderie provided by his shrewd, intelligent brothers. No man is an island.

Heinze will build the smelter he has determined is so necessary for the copper titan. He will also acquire the relatively insignificant Rarus mine (which he had leased for a time in order to study its workings), and through this seemingly modest conduit will secure a great fortune. By applying the apex law of mining, which holds that a miner is entitled to all mineral veins flowing from the apex or opening of those veins at the ground level, even if those veins are located in another owner's mine, Heinze will raid the Boston and Montana's Michael Davitt mine to the tune of $1 million in ore (a conservative estimate). By the time the major financiers back east could see what hit them, the trap has been sprung, the hand well played. Heinze had law and precedent on his side, as well as unstinting shamelessness, an undervalued virtue for capitalists. The inevitable legal proceedings would follow, suit and countersuit, but Heinze would prevail in court, largely because he had an excellent working relationship with Silver Bow County judges. In K. Ross Toole's brilliant formulation, ". . . how did you deal with a corrupt district judge in the tough city of Butte with eggs in his beard and larceny in his heart?"

But Heinze is now playing with the very big boys indeed, the Standard Oil trust that had acquired Daly's Anaconda and formed the Amalgamated Copper Company. Consider the odds of this clever, attractive, unscrupulous young man (he's just 31 at the turn of the century) defeating the greatest financial colossus the world has ever seen. And yet for a time he will pull it off. Part of his genius will be knowing when to throw in his lot with a rival, none other than William Andrews Clark, the severe, self-interested, impatient man who had arrived in Montana in 1862 as a goldminer and risen to enormous wealth. Clark and Heinze will find common cause in stacking the Montana legislature to (at last) enable Clark to become a senator, while Heinze needs control of the Silver Bow County courts to maintain his edge over the powerful trust. If anything, Clark has more at stake in the bargain than Heinze, for he has been denied entry to the Senate for bribing Montana legislators to name him senator in 1899. Humiliated to the core, Clark realizes he can only ascend to that long-cherished perch if he purchases votes in advance of the legislature's being seated. Poor Daly is dying at the age of 59 in New York City as these events unfold in faraway Montana— he must know his chief rival will at last realize the goal that has eluded him since that failed election of 1888, yet there's nothing to be done: Marcus Daly dies November 13, 1900. The surviving titans conspire on another scheme that yields immediate benefit: They adopt the eight-hour work day for their miners, effectively converting Standard Oil into the workingman's bane when the colossus refuses to follow suit.

Heinze also uses that most modern method of all for converting enemies into friends and allies: mass media, including public speeches and newspapers. His gift for oratory will serve him especially well in 1903 when labor unions offer to buy out his company in a bid to end the war with Amalgamated that is costing miners lives (pitched battles underground as competing veins cross paths) and money (forced into layoff by a vengeful mega-company that realizes labor alone could cow bold Heinze). Fritz stands before the assembled out-of-work miners, stating his case, winning their support and adoration:

> These people are my enemies—fierce, bitter, implacable. But they are your enemies, too. If they crush me today, they will crush you tomorrow.
>
> They will cut your wages.
>
> They will raise the tariff in their company stores on every bite you eat and every rag you wear. . . .
>
> . . . . They will force you to dwell in Standard Oil houses while you live—and they will bury you in Standard Oil coffins when you die!
>
> You and I are partners and allies. We stand—or fall—together.

Of course the miners cheer and back Heinze for the time being.

Newspapers are another required weapon in the battle for a copper empire. Daly launches his *Anaconda Standard*, housed in the company town he built to accommodate his smelter operations, the very month Heinze arrives in Butte. By January, 1900, Daly will task the *Standard*'s editor with investigating the annoying, litigious Fritz, whom he characterizes as "a blackmailer, a thief and a most dangerous and harmfull [sic] man to the business and property interests of Butte." Clark will put the *Butte Miner* to similar uses, along with many other newspapers he controls for purposes of personal propaganda. Heinze claims the *Reveille* as his journalistic vehicle, and the brash paper mirrors its cocky owner. In fact, his personal newspaper publishes his brilliant speech to the miners, amplifying its reach and impact.

For all his moxie and good luck, Fritz Heinze will face a foe far more powerful and persistent than he. Standard Oil creates the Amalgamated Mining Company with the clear, unmistakable objective of controlling all copper production in the United States. Butte is only the first of many battles for this fierce foe. Clark will abandon Heinze when it no longer serves his political ambitions, so the younger man will be left to battle the giant combination on his own. The 1903 shutdown of its operations, a terrifying action that lasts eighteen days, will convince Joseph Toole, the state's governor, to call a special session of the legislature that will enable Amalgamated to move its lawsuits to a Helena court, far from the reach of pro-Heinze judges. Having freed themselves from the arbitrary rulings of Butte courts, Amalgamated will put increasing pressure on Heinze to sell out to the combine. As Otto Heinze will recall of the forces converging on his brother,

> No one human being could carry the weight of this war upon his shoulders for an indefinite period, against the unending power of money, controlled by H. H. Rogers [head of Standard Oil] and his associates. With every year it cost more and more money and, in the end . . . if no compromise could be reached, it was bound to break down any human being mentally or financially, the more so if not loyally supported by the people of Montana and the miners of Butte.

On Valentine's Day, 1906, newspapers will report that F. Augustus Heinze has sold his Butte mining properties and equipment to Amalgamated for the princely sum of $12 million. It may have been the last happy day of his life.

The gifted fighter will reap the bitter fruits of his victory over the next eight years and suffer an early, undignified death. How

could that young man who detrains in Butte in 1889 be dead
by 1914? Though famous for its sulfurous air and soul-crushing
hard work, Butte had been a life source for Heinze. When he
leaves behind his mining youth and turns his attention to banking, he loses on many levels. He proves a reckless, ill-informed
investor in financial deals. Amalgamated lends its hand to his
demise, surreptitiously weakening his financial position when
opportunity allows, but the catastrophe is of Heinze's own making. His death will be attributed to cirrhosis of the liver. Such
can be the fate of the gifted, precocious youth, the jazz man who
improvises, fights, feints, and steals, his energies depleted by the
vicious contest of life fueled by the grand ambitions of the wide-
open days of American capitalism.

OCTOBER

In which Sarah Bickford rises in Virginia City, Teddy Blue Abbott begins marriage to Mary Stuart, and Cap Higgins' passing inspires Missoula's largest funeral.

The grand jury at its recent session in Deer Lodge found indictments against William H. Tracy for stealing a check from the agent of the Northern Pacific railroad at Elliston on the 26th of last August; Frank Beaudet for an assault with intent to rape one Leonie Fourney, a child eight years of age, at Champion; Fritz Shroeder for burglarizing the dwelling house of Catherine Glover at Avon; George Edwards, Matthew Granham and Frank Abbott for horsestealing—five indictments; George Upham, stealing; Grant Galoid, assault with intent to do bodily harm upon John Goddard; Cornelius Sullivan, assault with intent to murder John Mays; John Crawford, horse stealing; John Tighe, cattle stealing; Maud Whelan, assault with knife (in Granite) upon Esther Pierce, with intent to do bodily harm; Wm. H. Vennedy, embezzlement; Fritz Glover, larceny; Nick Kobalin, assault upon his wife with intent to kill.

CAN YOU IMAGINE IT, A FORMER FEMALE SLAVE TURNED owner of the Virginia City Water Company? Think how far she would have to come in space, time, and opportunity to achieve such a thing. Think of the layers of prejudice and resistance she would have to beat back constantly in her waking hours, in her dreams.

Sarah Bickford arrived in Virginia City as the servant to a judge's family in 1870. What did she see when she landed in that remote valley, altered by years of aggressive pan and industrial mining, prone to bitter cold winters and stark hot summers, as well as lingering hard feelings between Republicans and Democrats over the status of blacks? She carried memories of her slave years, born into that status in 1852 and owned (owned!) by one of the most prominent citizens of Jonesville, Tennessee, John Blair III. Blair had increased his wealth dramatically through the California gold rush of 1849. Bickford family stories tell that Sarah's parents were sold away during the Civil War and she was never to see them again, one of many scars from the peculiar institution.

Following the war and her emancipation, Sarah joined the Gammon family and adopted their name as her own. She accompanied the liberal lawyer John Murphy on his move from Tennessee to Montana to serve as Chief Justice for the Territory of Montana, working as nanny for his two stepchildren. Though Justice Murphy was to retreat to Tennessee after a short stay, Sarah would live out the rest of her days in this far western place. She may well have sensed freedom from formal, constricted roles in the informal western town, much as other women such as Clara McAdow and Nannie Alderson will report. Sarah married a black man, John Brown, in 1872, and they had three children together. The marriage proved another challenge to a young woman who had already endured so much: In 1880, she sued for divorce from Brown due to spousal abuse. Freedom from a bad marriage could not spare Sarah one of the hardest lots of all for a mother: She lived through the death of all three children by her first marriage.

One of the mysteries of life remains the perseverance of some while others go down to defeat at the hands of disappointment and prejudice. Sarah possessed more than common grit. In 1883, she married Stephen Bickford, a white man originally from

Sarah Bickford.

Maine who suffered poor health but seems to have been a loving husband and father. Stephen met Sarah when she cleaned his cabin, suggestive of a western disregard for class barriers to marriage. Most importantly for Sarah's future well-being, he wrote a will in 1887 that guaranteed his property would be passed on to her, a generous and uncommon act that hints Sarah had learned hard-won lessons from her years of dealing with a legal system that marginalized a black woman's rights.

Despite his health struggles, Bickford purchased two-thirds control of the Virginia City Water Company in 1888. His wife aided him as a chief accountant, preparing her to manage the business. When Stephen dies from pneumonia in 1900, she will be well-positioned to take control of the company. But that control will not come easily: Sarah will have to prove all of Bickford's debts have been paid before she can officially claim majority ownership of the Virginia City Water Company. Shrewdly, she later will purchase the final third, taking full control, and will move her office to the notorious building where five presumed road agents were hanged on January 14, 1864, an event witnessed by the precocious, horrified Mollie Sheehan.

Bickford's story illustrates the small but important African American presence in early Montana. The U. S. Census gives only a partial account of that role: The number of blacks rises from 183 in 1870 to 1,490 in 1890. But these figures almost certainly represent an undercounting. Even so, Bickford, along with other early arrivals in the region, will hold her own in a territory that prevents African Americans from voting. One of the evident benefits of statehood is federal law requires that black men be allowed to vote, even as the newly adopted constitution deprives women of that right. Still, in 1909 the Montana Legislature will outlaw mixed-race marriages, an onerous act that will remain in place until 1953. Sarah lived at a moment of historical possibility that will prove contingent, temporary, and subject to the whims of biased citizens. Putting that possibility to use, Sarah will build a life that has been recognized by induction into the Gallery of Outstanding Montanans in the Montana State Capitol Rotunda.

THEY MOVE INTO THEIR NEW HOME ON OCTOBER 6, THE OPEN range cowboy and his mixed-raced wife, daughter of the famous Granville Stuart and his Shoshone spouse, Awbonnie. It's a union of one of those loose-limbed, free-spirited riders on the plains, so scandalous and romantic, with what amounts to Montana royalty. Teddy Blue Abbott and Mary Stuart build a ranch and a bond that will endure until her death nearly eighty years later.

Teddy had been one of the original open range cowboys, coming north from Texas in the 1870s with herds driven out of a state overrun with livestock following the Civil War. He was born with high spirits and a taste for fun, a perfect combination for a young man riding from the Red River to Miles City. The son of a disaffected, judgmental British emigrant father, Teddy found freedom and a world of play on those long drives north. He recognized the hard work, too, and the real dangers of lightning storms and badger holes and antagonistic Indians. Yet he would tell Charlie Russell, a good friend from the moment they met on the range near Moccasin, Montana, that he wishes he could have lived like an Indian, a true pastoral life, simple and unfettered. Russell memorably replies, "Ted, there's a pair of us. They've been living in heaven for a thousand years, and we took it away from 'em for forty dollars a month."

Teddy acquired his famous nickname during one of many incidents in the wide-open cow town of Miles City. As he followed a potential paramour backstage at the theater, it dawned on him that he may be set up for a robbery (he was making 75 dollars a month, a good wage for a cowboy at the time). As he turned to flee the feared hold up, "my spur caught on a carpet and I fell through a thin partition onto the stage. Well, I thought, if you're

Teddy Blue Abbott, his wife Mary and their five children, and Mary's brother, Edward Stuart, 1902. MONTANA HISTORICAL SOCIETY RESEARCH CENTER PHOTO-GRAPH ARCHIVES, HELENA, MONTANA

before an audience you've got to do something, so I grabbed a chair from one of the musicians and straddled it and bucked it all around the stage, yelling, 'Whoa, Blue! Whoa, Blue!'—which was a cowpuncher expression at the time. . . . And when I went out of that theatre that night I was Blue, and Teddy Blue I have been for fifty-five years.'"

In many ways, then, Teddy became the source and inspiration for the cowboy myth that endures until this day. His stories provide a source text for the glamorized images circulating in film and fiction. Yet in many ways he worked hard to undercut the romance. He emphasized the youth, physical danger, and sheer stupidity of his peers. As his conversation with Russell revealed, he acknowledged and even mourned the eclipse of indigenous people, ruminating on how the U.S. destroyed the great bison herds as a put-up job on the Indians. These are not passing moments in his extended narrative—they are highpoints, italicized and emphatic. Perhaps even more surprisingly, Teddy wrote that he dreamed of owning his own place early in his time on the trail, recognizing his open range cattle drive days as a prelude to something permanent and stable. The romance of the range would prove a brief interlude even for one of its most compelling living symbols.

Perhaps that's why Blue goes out of his way to praise Granville Stuart as ranch manager and vigilante leader. For all the stress and strain of Mary's falling out with her father in June of 1889 over his fixation on Belle, Teddy appreciates all that the father had done to make it possible for the young cowhand (he's only 29 when he marries) to set himself up on a ranch. By Teddy's account, Stuart treated his cowboys well, not only respecting them as laborers but encouraging them to buy their own cattle to make a start on building their future. Blue claimed to act as a key go-between during the lynching days on the range, and he pulled no punches: He unequivocally defended the actions of the extralegal posse, recreating the threat posed by renegades concealed in the broken terrain and isolated hangouts of north-central Montana. The young cowboy may well have felt that Stuart was not only protecting the DHS holdings but the future hopes of a man who dreamt of running his own herd.

Blue also offers a dramatic rendering of the Stuart family, describing an assemblage of intense human beings who created a remarkable life for themselves in the outback of Montana. The memoirist goes out of his way to debunk the myth of the loneliness and isolation of ranches, asserting that the large Stuart family, sharing the ranch with Reece Anderson's clan, carried on a lively, fulfilling, often sophisticated life. It's clear that Teddy was charmed and even a bit intimidated by the world he discovered on the DHS. By his account the Stuart daughters—Katie, Mary, and Lizzie—were well dressed, well educated, and poised. Given his previous dealings with women, such as the one he encountered on the night he gained his nickname, the Stuart daughters must have been impressive indeed. Add to that mix the strength and moral force of Awbonnie, whom Blue admires, and you have the makings of an attractive family that would act as a perfect magnet for a footloose cowboy longing for permanence.

Of course, even as he praises the Shoshone mother, he acknowledges how she put up roadblocks to Mary and Teddy's courting. Perhaps the mother saw in Teddy a frisky young man with few prospects for supporting her daughters, and after all, Awbonnie had lived out the consequences of Granville's restless search for wealth. Perhaps the mother also sensed the changes in Montana culture that made mixed-race wives suspect, disrespected, marginal, and so was cautious about sanctioning a marriage that could expose one of her daughters to a long life of ridicule and casual cruelty. In a sense, she was simply acting on the moral norms of late-Victorian culture, for Granville himself was careful to monitor the couple's time together, making sure they went their separate ways in the evening.

When Mary and Teddy take up their new residence on October 6, then, their union follows a long courtship of more than two years, the loss of Awbonnie and Katie, and Granville's drift toward a new family, a new life. Mary insists on an elopement rather than a formal wedding ceremony: "They wanted us to get married at the D H S, but at the last minute she got an independent streak and so we drove over to the town of Alpine, with the Anderson girls and a neighbor, and we were married by a justice of the peace. . . . And that in a way writes the end to the story of my life on the open range ."

Despite the nearly elegiac tone of that last sentence, Teddy expresses utter joy at his change of status, though the couple's original house would never qualify as a fetching place: "After we were married our first home was a ranch we rented and then bought from a man who had moved to the state of Washington. It had a poor frame house, too cold to winter in, and I will never forget our first night on that ranch. . . . [W]e only had my cowpuncher's bed laid on the floor, while Mary always had had a nice bed at home and plenty of everything. The pack rats ran over us, and the little girl sure hugged up tight." Teddy will note with pride as he tells his story to Helena Huntington Smith that in defiance of this humble beginning, he can claim $50,000 in the bank, a substantial grubstake for a man who began as a carefree cowboy on the western range in the 1870s. And Mary and Teddy's rupture with Granville will heal in time, leaving moving memories of the aging grandfather playing with the children of that union formalized in the fall of 1889.

IT IS THE LEAST THEY CAN DO FOR THE MAN WHO STARTED IT all, Cap Higgins, who began building Missoula Mills in November of 1864 with Frank Worden and David Pattee. And now his time has come, the time that comes for all men, his passing over into the afterlife, and by God, there would be a good show, the

Capt. Christopher Power Higgins. Montana Historical Society Research Center Photograph Archives, Helena, Montana

biggest funeral in the history of this town located at the nexus of five valleys:

> Yesterday Missoula was the scene of the largest funeral procession ever seen in this vicinity. At 2 o'clock the Masons, the Valley Rifles, fire company, and hundreds of friends assembled at the residence of the late Capt. Higgins to perform the last sad rites over all that was mortal of that noble and highly esteemed gentleman.

Cap had earned that affection, that respect, through his years of building Missoula. He served in the Army back in the 1850s with Isaac Stevens, governor of Washington Territory, who was surveying for a railroad and conducting treaty negotiations with the tribal nations. After starting the sawmill and gristmill back in 1864 near where the Rattlesnake flows into the Clark Fork River, he founded the Missoula National Bank to capitalize the many enterprises that would no doubt follow in this perfectly positioned town. That town watched as he and his lovely wife, daughter of the famed Richard Grant, Hudson Bay Company factor, raised nine children. Cap's whistle calling his children home for lunch became legendary as "the noon whistle." Perhaps most importantly, Higgins helped assure the Northern Pacific Railroad would route its line through Missoula in 1883, the absolutely necessary link for the town's survival. Cap gave away many town lots to the railroad to sweeten the inducement. Yes, the people of Missoula, not just the estimated 600 who attend his funeral, have reason to love this man.

In attendance that day, though probably not calling attention to himself, must be Andrew B. Hammond, Higgins' chief rival for control of Missoula's economy and future. It would be hard to imagine two more dissimilar personalities struggling for dominance in a still-raw Montana town. If Cap seemed ever the merry Irishman with a taste for conversation and good stories, Hammond is the model of the new capitalist, determined,

A. B. Hammond. MANSFIELD LIBRARY ARCHIVES AND SPECIAL COLLEC-
TIONS, MISSOULA, MONTANA

self-centered, and effective. He had come up through the school
of hard knocks, first in the timber industry of New Brunswick,
then as a wood hawk on the upper Missouri at a time when
Lakota often murdered these providers of fuel for the steam-
boats. When Hammond landed in Missoula in 1872, he must
have taken a look around and realized opportunity was truly at
hand. Never one to wait his turn or defer to elders, Hammond
cast his eye on a resource so rich, so overwhelmingly available,
so manifestly graspable that even this seemingly unsentimental
man must have shed a tear or let out a sigh at the prospect. Timber. The very thing he had come of age harvesting surrounded
him on land of uncertain (to his eyes) jurisdiction. It would not
take long for Hammond to align his interests with monied men
such as Edward Bonner and Richard Eddy to begin harvesting
and milling that lumber for the apparently unending demand
from the railroads and the mining industry blowing up in Butte.

Unlike other early emigrants, Hammond's political affiliation
was changeable, not fixed by the still-traumatic Civil War and
the bitter residue, both military and personal, of that fighting.
When the time came for a change of party, he made the move
with straightforward logic, unsentimental calculation. If Cap
Higgins had long been a loyal Democrat, his rival would find a
way to convert to Republican in 1888, and for very good reasons.
The federal government under Democratic leadership brought
suit against him and his partners (including one Marcus Daly)
for illegally harvesting timber on federal and Indian lands. By
any reasonable reckoning, the government had Hammond dead
to rights, for he seemed to care not a whit for petty concerns
such as public ownership of the land. He saw profit, unending
profit, in those trees, gifted to him as though by God, and he had
little patience for the niceties of the common wealth. Hammond
was the real deal, the laissez faire capitalist who believed he was
entitled to marshal those resources for his personal benefit and
the benefit of a growing Montana.

And so it was that Hammond switched party affiliation to support the candidacy of Thomas Carter, Republican, over and against one of the big players, William Clark, in the 1888 election, leading to the rift between Clark and Daly that would plague Montana for the next twelve years. Clark was not the first early emigrant in the region to suffer such an indignity. Cap Higgins had often felt the sting of Hammond's cold mind, as when the younger man forced the town founder out of control of his own bank, the Missoula National, in a ruthless takeover that Hammond could justify as the necessary act of a responsible businessman displacing a careless banker prone to making loans based on personal affection. (Higgins had a great deal in common with Sam Hauser, it would seem.) No wonder Higgins was in the process of creating a new bank at the time of his death. But Hammond had slighted the founder in an even more powerful and direct way. Though Higgins could be credited with enticing the Northern Pacific to build its line through Missoula, he would lose to Hammond the contract for timber to build the railroad.

Hammond became known as "the Octopus," the man with tentacles controlling multiple businesses in Missoula, the new state, the region. He can be credited with helping form the Missoula Mercantile Company, a legendary institution created, in part, to shield him from lawsuits against his logging practices on public and reservation lands. Hammond also helped capitalize and feed the famous Bonner mills to the east of Missoula. Yet one would be hard pressed to find any evidence of the man in today's Garden City. In part, that's due to his leaving behind Montana in the 1890s to pursue the much bigger prize of timber sales in Oregon and California. In larger part, it can be attributed to Hammond's take-no-prisoners style in a region that seemed to favor the more personal touch of a Cap Higgins to the ruthless, if highly efficient, workings of a capitalist's mind. Cap's whistle is still a legend in Missoula, but Hammond's straight-ahead, unyielding stare wins few friends or cherished memories. Yet perhaps the harder man wins the race of life in the end, for Cap Higgins' heirs will squander his fortune, leaving only kind recollections and lingering respect as the Irishman's legacy.

NOVEMBER

In which Charlo consents to leave his home in the Bitterroot, Montana's new status takes on a bitter taste, Frank Linderman objects to statehood, and Evelyn and Ewen Cameron honeymoon in the Terry badlands.

Deep down in the gloomy depths of the St. Lawrence mine, a thousand feet from the surface, buried in the sump, lie the bodies of two, if not four brave men, who risked and lost their lives in an attempt to suppress a fire on the 500-foot level early yesterday morning. The names of these men are Patrick Murphy, Henry Page, Jerry Sullivan and Tim Kelleher.

LET THIS BE THE DAY, THEN, LET THIS BE THE DAY. AFTER almost twenty years of telling the Americans no, after so many feints and refusals, after honoring his father Victor's strategies to keep his people in the Bitterroot Valley, let November 3, 1889, be the day. Charlo, chief of the Bitterroot Salish, relents and says yes to a move to the Jocko Valley:

> I will go—I and my children. My young men are becoming bad; they have no place to hunt. My women are hungry. For their sake I will go. I do not want the land you promise. I do not believe in your promises. All I want is enough ground for my grave. We will go over there.

What choice does he have? Withering crops; near-starvation; disease; the relentless influx of emigrants (Marcus Daly owns a

Charlo, chief of the Bitterroot Salish. Mansfield Library Archives and Special Collections, Missoula, Montana

22,000-acre ranch in the heart of the Bitterroot); the numbing persistence of Indian agent Peter Ronan; General Carrington's refusal to accept no; and yes, the death of Arlee, the Salish sub-chief who accepted the American bribe in 1872 and moved many of the people to the Jocko, against Charlo's opposition. Now that Arlee is dead, Charlo can take his people north with a modicum of honor. In no way would he be perceived as respecting the choices of that enemy within, and he would be chief over all the Salish once again.

Victor negotiated wisely and well in 1855 when he insisted that his people could remain in the Bitterroot until the president conducted a proper survey and made a formal determination of whether the land belonged to the Salish. The maneuver frustrated Isaac Stevens, territorial governor who was in a hurry to complete agreements with the many nations in then-Washington Territory to secure passageway for roads and, ultimately, railroads. The treaty was ratified by Congress in 1859, yet no survey had been completed. Instead, in 1872, James Garfield, an experienced congressman from Ohio who would later be assassinated early in his term as president, journeyed to the Bitterroot to negotiate the Salishes' final exodus to the Jocko. Offering land, farm implements, and chief status as inducements, Garfield was able to divide the leaders. Arlee accepted the offer and led members of the nation to the land north of Missoula, causing a permanent rupture with Charlo.

Peter Ronan reports that in 1889 Charlo's band includes 176 men, women, and children. The agent describes the drought conditions in harrowing terms: "The outlook for the Indians this year is gloomy in the extreme. The drought of the summer has been unknown to the oldest Indians. The country is parched and the usually luxuriant bunch grass is burned to the roots on prairie and upland." Ronan's report makes it clear that Charlo is not alone in his resistance to civilizing tactics, for he writes peevishly,

Owing to the prejudices of the several chiefs and of head-
men of the tribes, a large majority of the Indians of the
Flathead Reservation are yet averse to taking of land in
severalty under the act of Congress which became a law
on the 8th of February, 1887. The older members of the
tribes, and also the young men who have not yet received
any of the advantages of education, go to swell the majority against land in severalty, because they are loath to give
up their savage customs. They say at councils and at their
fireside talks that the residue of the land will be sold by
the Government to white settlers, thus breaking up their
reservation and mixing the Indians up promiscuously
with the whites.

The Confederated Tribes will prove prescient, of course, since
the Dawes Act will unfold exactly as they predict, for large por-
tions of the land promised to them forever will enter into white
ownership. Charlo's distrust of the Americans is well-founded,
then, and he never expressed that doubt more eloquently than
in 1883, when speaking with Senator George Vest of Missouri,
who had traveled to Stevensville to complete Garfield's work:

You may carry me to Fort Missoula dead, but you will
never carry me there alive. I heard before that your great
father had printed a book showing my name to the treaty
[of 1872], but I never signed nor told anybody else to sign
it for me.

As to carrying me to the fort like a bag of grain, you did
not talk that way when your people were going to California and came through my country sick and hungry. I
had many warriors then and could have killed them all,
but we nursed and fed them and did all we could to make
them happy.

Nearly all my warriors are dead now, and I have only women and children. You have your foot on my head now. . . but then I had my foot on your head.

There is not a drop of white blood on the hands of my people. . . .

I have no faith in what you say now, for the government has broken all the promises made by your great father in 1855.

Ironically, Charlo's acceptance of the exodus will not lead to his removal from the Bitterroot for two years, resulting in near-starvation when, in anticipation of the move, the Salish do not plant crops. In October, 1891, they will march solemnly from their home ground near St. Mary's Mission, through the Missoula valley, north to the Flathead Reservation. All this had been—still remains—Salish land, and no bill, no treaty, no forced march can change that. No wonder Mary Ann Coombs, a ten-year-old Salish girl at the time of the removal, will recall "everyone was in tears, even the men" and the procession was similar to "a funeral march." The agent's wife, Mary, will report that Charlo proved stoic and defiant after his removal to the agency near the present-day town of Arlee. A new house and proffered land could never erase the bitterness of that parting from his homeland.

THAT THE ANNOUNCEMENT OF REALIZED STATEHOOD was received by every citizen of Montana with a sense of joy, is a fact that needs no defending. That, with the feeling of rejoicing there is mingled a sentiment of regret over the unhappy complications involving peace and good order among the people, is a truth that need not be recited. That a plot to steal the new state and pervert the popular will has made itself dangerous by mere force of self-assertion is admitted. That the patriotic people of Montana will resist the insidious assaults of crime is as certain as is the conviction that its people love liberty and prize the blessings which follow Montana's welcome as the forty-first star in the galaxy of states.

Thus the *Anaconda Standard,* Marcus Daly's personal newspaper, born in September of this very year, proclaims Montana's admission as the 41st state on November 8. The newspaper is of a piece with the town Daly built as a model of paternalistic capitalism, home for the smelters and their workers that process the vast quantities of copper extracted from Butte's mines. No wonder Daly originally named the town "Copperopolis"! Just this year, Daly's famed Montana Hotel, a model of elegance, opened its doors with a splendid ball on July 4, the very day the Constitutional Convention commenced in Helena. Daly is already dreaming his new town will become the state capital. Yet the *Standard,* a vehicle for the Democratic Party, is hardly unmixed in its praise for statehood, an event so long desired by citizens of the territory. What could possibly temper enthusiasm for ascent to full, enfranchised status in the expanding nation?

Similar to the first territorial legislature in 1864, the first state legislature is a house divided. The Senate is evenly split between eight Democrats and eight Republicans. The situation in the House is far more fraught. Disputes over voting irregularities in one of Silver Bow County's districts results in a knockdown, drag-out fight over whether to seat five Republicans or Democrats in the lower chamber. The outcome would not only shape the state's inaugural legislation but would determine the party affiliation of Montana's first senators, for in 1889, U. S. senators are chosen by state legislatures.

Surely common sense, or the courts, or leaders such as Joseph K. Toole, first state governor, could break this impasse. But such

Anaconda, Montana, 1887. MONTANA HISTORICAL SOCIETY RESEARCH CENTER PHOTOGRAPH ARCHIVES, HELENA, MONTANA

is not to be. The twenty-five years of bitter partisan wrangling between two political parties, an original sin born in the crucible of the Civil War and the creation of a territory by a controversial President Lincoln, culminates in the absurd scene of two Houses meeting separately, one Democratic, the other Republican. While each advances legislation for consideration by the Senate, the divided upper chamber is unable to pass those bills. Even more shamefully, each forwards candidates for Senate to the U. S. Congress: the Republicans propose Wilbur Sanders and T. C. Power, while the Democrats propose William Andrews Clark and Martin Maginnis (defeated in his bid to serve as the first Montana Congressman by none other than Thomas Carter, the very man who defeated Clark in 1888!).

What a roll call of important political figures in early Montana. Sanders, vigilante, lawyer, defender of rights for Indians and Chinese, and a relentless, remorseless Republican, could be on the cusp of one of his most coveted rewards for all his years of service on behalf of his party. Power established a trading empire centered in Fort Benton that serves the prairies north and south. Martin Maginnis had been an extraordinarily influential nonvoting delegate to Congress for twelve years and exercised vital influence toward assuring the Great Northern Railway's passage through Indian lands in 1887.

As for Clark, his selection by the (quite possibly) illegitimate Democratic Montana House marks another step on his tortured journey toward serving in Congress. Following that bitter defeat the year before at the hands of Daly and A. B. Hammond, one might have supposed his ardor for service has cooled. But that would prove a vast underestimation of his vanity. So dissimilar to Charles Broadwater and Daly, who eschew pursuit of elective office, Clark seems to need the validation of his status through a Senate seat. Unquestionably a brilliant, disciplined businessman, his precise, practical, focused mind seems to go out of focus and lose perspective when it comes to the idea of a Senate

Martin Maginnis, taken when he was a delegate to the Montana Constitutional Convention, 1889. MONTANA HISTORICAL SOCIETY RESEARCH CENTER PHOTOGRAPH ARCHIVES, HELENA, MONTANA

Thomas C. Power. MONTANA HISTORICAL SOCIETY RESEARCH CENTER
PHOTOGRAPH ARCHIVES, HELENA, MONTANA

seat. In the end he will be accused (for good reasons) of buying a seat at the turn of the century, but for now, in 1889, he pins his hopes on the unlikely possibility the U. S. Senate will choose to seat Montana's Democratic slate.

What a comedy of errors, a carnival of folly for the new state. More than one national political leader must wonder whether twenty-five years has been a sufficient incubation period for Montana's statehood. The two Montana Houses and competing slates of senators make for good fodder in newspapers all over the country, clearly relishing evidence of the new state's unfitness for its new status. As for the *Anaconda Standard*, the Democratic newspaper consistently lobbies for admission of neither set of senators, arguing that the Montana Legislature has not been properly constituted and therefore cannot legally appoint senators. Recognizing the odds are long for appointment of Clark and Maginnis, given the makeup of the U. S. Senate, the newspaper seeks to stop any appointment at all. At the same time, the newspaper is proud to tout the virtues of the Democratic pair: "The Standard was the first newspaper in the United States to come to the front with the declaration that all four senators picked out in Helena ought to be sent back to Montana by the upper house in Washington. . . . As far as candidates go, the democratic party will never present two better men than Clark and Maginnis. They would grace the exalted office of senator, Montana would be proud of them. There are no railroad ties that bind them, no land-grab mud sticks to their overshoes."

In classic journalistic style of the era, the newspaper asserts the virtue of Democratic claimants by defaming the Republicans. Mention of "railroad ties" (fine pun) and "land-grab" refers to the contention Sanders and Power are in the pocket of the Northern Pacific Railroad, seeking to hold on to its massive land grant from 1864 in order to control the lucrative mineral rights. "Disingenuous" seems hardly adequate to describe the *Standard*'s assertions, given Maginnis' very public embrace of the Great Northern's land grab in northern Montana in 1887 and 1888. Ethics are also somewhat problematic for Mr. Clark, who never shies from spreading a bit of cash to support his electoral chances.

In the end, of course, the Republican Senate does what expedient politicians always do: They choose Wilbur Sanders and Tom Power as Montana's first senators. The *Standard* takes that selection as the occasion to unpack some of its most unrestrained prose: "The robbery of Montana was completed this afternoon at 5:45 o'clock. The stolen seats will be occupied tomorrow by Sanders and Power. . . . With uplifted hands they swore to defend the constitution that had been trampled upon to seat them."

FRANK LINDERMAN BELIEVES THE OLD TRAPPER, ALVIN LEE, when he objects to Montana's newly-minted statehood, "Now she's gone to hell." In 1885, Linderman bought a ticket for $67.50 from Chicago to Missoula, as far as the Northern Pacific would run. He had a simple, irrepressible goal: Get to the real West, the West of Indians and fur trapping, before it was gone. It's a familiar impulse in Montana and the West in general, one acted out at dude ranches and other temporary getaways, but Linderman went all in, striving to become the mountain man of his dreams. No wonder statehood sounded like hell—civilization and regulation and more imposition on the Indians.

When he arrived at Flathead Lake in 1885, Linderman set about fully inhabiting his new persona, determined to live off the land and commune with the Indians. His impulse was exactly that stated by Teddy Blue Abbott: He wanted to become an Indian. That would be the theme of his life, and that drive led to remarkable literary and political achievements, though Linderman is strangely undervalued in Montana folklore. But first he had to test his mettle and find a way to survive in what he considered the last wilderness in America, the land around Flat-

Frank B. Linderman. Montana Historical Society Research Center Photograph Archives, Helena, Montana

head Lake. His clumsy efforts led to the predictable and at times laughable mistakes of all greenhorns attempting to shed years of training (though he was only 16) to reclaim a direct physical relationship with the natural world: "I had had the bad luck, while building the cabin, to step squarely upon the upturned edge of the sharp axe, dropped in tenderfoot fashion among some limbs that had been trimmed from the cabin logs. . . . [T]he wound dampened my ardor so much that when my partners left me I felt mighty blue." Yet he persisted and even thrived, becoming close to Cree and Salish Indians living nearby, mastering the skills of the trapper, and relishing his long jaunts in the stunning mountains of northwest Montana.

It couldn't last. Love will intervene in the form of an attractive young woman, Minnie Mae Johns, met quite by chance in Demersville, the region's largest town until it is eclipsed by Kalispell when the Great Northern arrives. He will be forced to choose between his footloose atavistic life and making a living to support a family. When he leaves the woods for marriage and standard work, Linderman will launch upon a series of jobs that connect him to a full range of Montana landscapes and people. One will take him to Butte, the industrial mining colossus, where he works as an assayer, an assessor of valuable metal content. It's difficult to imagine a starker contrast than that between Flathead Lake and the tough, loud, polluted, colorful, roiling city on a hill: "Sometimes, especially in damp weather, the whole of Butte City was hidden by sulphurous smoke and acrid fumes so completely that it was not uncommon for men on their way to work to lose their direction. . . . Trolley cars spluttered green flashes of sulphurous light; and funeral processions were all too common in the days of Butte's 'stink-piles.'" Here Linderman refers to the open-heap roasting piles used to smelt copper, creating arsenic and sulphur dioxide fumes that blanket Butte. William Clark famously argues during the 1889 Constitutional Convention (with apparent sincerity) that the foul air is good for ladies' complexions and therefore an acceptable by-product of the mining and smelting industrial complex. Unfortunately, Linderman will link Butte's catastrophic environment to the influx of foreign-born workers, revealing a hardcore nativism that cuts against the grain of his deep sympathy for indigenous peoples.

A series of hit-and-miss jobs follow Linderman's Butte years in places such as Sheridan, where he will take up assaying once again and will add newspaper work to the mix. He will serve as Assistant Secretary of State for two years, no doubt planting the seeds of political ambition that would lead to his losing campaign to Jeannette Rankin in the 1916 Republican primary. Linderman will attribute this humiliating loss to the "fad" of women's suffrage, hinting at discomfort with changes in women's status. He will at last hit a mother lode of affluence when he becomes an insurance agent operating out of Helena, covering the entire state of Montana. That job will not only fill his financial but his writing coffers, for much of his best work will be fed and inspired by his travels. He will become familiar with the tribal nations throughout the region and master Indian sign language, a critical skill for the life he is about to choose. He will commit himself fully to a writing life that will at least preserve and transmit native stories and a wilderness ethic. Perhaps in no other way is Linderman more typically Montanan than in his obsession with the writing life. He will later assert, "My literary efforts had failed. . . .But writing is a disease." Fortunately, those living a century after he put his words to paper can attest he was wrong—if the sales he so longed for eluded him, many of his books remain in print and carry much of the knowledge he longed to share.

Flush with money from his years as an insurance salesman, then, and longing for a return to his beloved Flathead country, Linderman will quit the insurance man's life in 1917 to pursue writing as a full-time vocation. And does he ever have stories to tell. Above all he wishes to convey the Indian stories before they are lost. His most important contributions will be the affecting, detailed, at times heart-breaking stories of Plenty Coups and Pretty Shield, participants in the last days of pre-reservation life for northern plains indigenous people. Linderman believes in the corrupting power of civilization and urges attention to stories of grounded peoples who can teach much about establishing an original, sustaining, meaningful relationship with the land. No wonder Linderman will be called one of the last Romantics.

Yet his efforts on behalf of his Indian friends and relatives—he is adopted into the Blackfeet, Chippewa, and Crow tribes—will go far beyond the merely sentimental, literary, or historical. He will work tirelessly for the establishment of an Indian reservation for the Chippewa and Cree peoples caught in the no-person's land following Riel's revolt:

> Claiming kinship with the Crees, and knowing nothing about the white man's line that divided the United States from Canada, these Chippewas had fought with the Crees in the Riel Rebellion against Canadian troops, so that, in a sense, they were outlaws with the Crees themselves. Both had adopted Montana as their home after the fighting across the line, neither doubting that they had as much right to remain here as anybody else. The history of the band, garbled to suit unfriendly white men, began to spread, making my task of bettering its condition more difficult.

This passionate defense emerges from Linderman's first year in Montana, for he met and befriended Cree Indians in flight from the failed fight in Saskatchewan, the very Cree who had fled across the Montana border seeking asylum: "How well I remember my first meeting with these Indians. I had seen them soon after their battle with Canadian troops at Duck Creek

[Duck Lake? Frog Creek?] in 1885. Some of them were wounded, and all had seemed to me to be upstanding men." Linderman's sympathy for the landless Indians is only compounded during his years in Helena, where he seeks food and shelter for old friends living on the edge of town, forced to live off garbage and offal, the castoff food of white society. His advocacy, linked to the work of many others, especially members of the Chippewa and Cree nations, will lead, at last, to creation of the Rocky Boy Reservation in 1916.

No wonder, then, twenty-year-old Linderman thinks Montana is going to hell when it becomes a state. All his ideals, all his experiences, all his passions teach him the wild is better than the civilized, the natural improves upon the technological, the people are more important than the companies and institutions, and stories are far greater than the numbers of industrialists and accountants. In an autobiographical fragment, he will assert with little ambiguity or doubt, "the white man is the natural enemy of all natural things. . . .The wilderness, my wilderness, did not last long. The railroad came to it, and then the country began to settle rapidly. The old days were forever ended for both the Indian and me." In this way Linderman challenges Turner's thesis, for salvation lies not in the adaptation of civilization to a wilderness condition but the complete renunciation of that civilization. Grounded in this dire view of modernity and progress, Linderman will oppose assimilationist policies such as allotment, urging the people of the Rocky Boy Reservation to reject attempts to subdivide their land into property subject to sale.

A young woman sits sidesaddle on her horse, tanned and relaxed, wearing the rough clothing of the hunt. Her horse is equipped for pursuing game, rifle and machete at the ready. She nonchalantly poses the head of a bear cub for the camera, a teasing, assured gesture, as though saying, "I'm as wild and untamed as this beast." The background landscape, while blurred and indistinct, speaks of wind, sun, and exposure. Who is this bold young woman, and what is she doing here? This is none other than Evelyn Jephson Cameron, twenty-one-year-old British woman from an elite family, on her honeymoon in the badlands of eastern Montana with her Scottish husband Ewen, fourteen years her senior. That photo captures the appeal and wonder of Montana for this daughter of British society and fore-shadows the strange, appealing life she would claim in one of the most remote regions of America. Evelyn Cameron will create a Montana of one's own.

Evelyn and Ewen's surprising choice of a honeymoon destina-tion tells much about their status, wealth, and desires. Evelyn is the energetic, bored daughter of an affluent family, weary of the rounds of socializing and pampering that define her life in Eng-land. Ewen, a kind of fallen Scottish king, lived in the remote parts of Scotland and favors bird-watching and hunting to more refined pursuits of the British gentry. He had been married to a renowned opera singer (in truth, he may not be legally divorced at the time of his journey to Montana with Evelyn). The Flowers did not favor this match, perplexed by Evelyn's perverse choice of a mate. The Camerons' up-and-down twenty-six-year mar-riage will give some credence to the family's doubts, yet Evelyn will never declare the match a failure.

The couple chooses eastern Montana for their honeymoon in part because Evelyn's beloved older brother, Percy, hunted in this very region years earlier. In that sense, the Camerons are follow-ing the path of many British elites who see the "wilds" of Mon-tana as an outlandish place to test their mettle, their fitness, their strength. The Camerons are hardly roughing it, however—they are accompanied by an English cook and one of Colonel George Armstrong Custer's scouts. Evelyn and Ewen will become part of an ex-pat community that bets heavily on the ranching boom of the 1880s and 90s, most often to see those investments come to naught, but charmed (at least temporarily) by life in the out-

Evelyn Cameron, holding a bear cub on her lap, 1890s. Montana Historical Society Research Center Photograph Archives, Helena, Montana

back. The Camerons will invest in a grand scheme to raise polo ponies for the British market, a seemingly can't-miss proposition that will strip them of capital and the hope for wealth. It will turn out that polo ponies cannot weather the seasickness of an Atlantic crossing, and so Ewen's best-laid plan will collapse. In the aftermath of that embarrassing failure, Evelyn will prove herself one of the hardiest of British transplants, a determined, practical, clever woman who will turn to boarders, gardening, ranch work, and photography to sustain her and her husband. Ewen will drift deeper into his eccentric obsessions, tracking exotic birds such as falcons and hawks and writing fulsome articles about them for British and American journals: ". . . Apart from the pleasant emotions, which the expectation of seeing game evokes, badlands derive a definite charm from their solitude and geological features. Miles may be traversed without finding sign of a human being or hearing sound more civilized than the howling of a wolf." Of course, Ewen has access to this "empty" place precisely because the bison have been eliminated and indigenous peoples have been removed to troubled reservations.

Meanwhile, Evelyn will make sure that Eve Ranch, which took on three incarnations in the course of their marriage, will run as efficiently as possible. There will be many inducements to return home, both financial and familial, yet Evelyn and Ewen will stick. After a year of exile in England in 1900-01, Evelyn will never be tempted by that option again. She has become unfit for an elite British life—her deeply tanned skin, lined face, and rough hands mark a woman most at home in the badlands. She will become an American citizen in tribute to her adopted country.

We know so much about Evelyn and Ewen in large part because of her photography. She made a settler's bet, a reach toward some means to keep Eve Ranch together when they were forced to live on Evelyn's modest remittance. Though somewhat aloof,

Evelyn was fascinated by people, and her eye for their character, cares, and need for recognition would yield a helpful income. A gifted contemporary Montana photographer, Kristi Hager, will observe that Cameron never condescended to her subjects, whatever the distance in upbringing. Indeed, Cameron's elite education allowed her to connect with some of her subjects in surprising ways—she could speak Italian and so would establish a special rapport with the Italian immigrants who worked on the train crews in her home region. Yet, Hager will point out there was always a bit of a twist, a surprising angle, light, or pose, that would prevent Evelyn's photographs from becoming merely conventional. Her fierce intelligence showed through in her posing an entire community in front of their few buildings, taking that panoramic photo from atop a train car. Or the memorable photograph of five women and four children, posed in the middle space between camera and badlands, hinting at the daunting conditions these loving parents must overcome to see their children through to adulthood.

Cameron would record the stark transformations of her home region in the Yellowstone River valley, especially with the arrival of the homesteaders in the early twentieth century. Like many who had lived long on the sere northern plains and knew well the challenge of making crops flourish in that unyielding climate, she worried about these newcomers, who seemed ill-equipped physically or mentally to turn buffalo grass into crops. Yet again, she did not demean or look down upon those emigrants, instead allowing the photographs to image their grit, pride, and hopefulness. These photographs will become a means to signify the homesteaders' accomplishments and acquisitions—the familiar shack, a Model T, livestock, and produce from the garden. These images seem to say, "We are here, we are alive—our labor matters, and you back home don't need to worry about us."

Of all her subjects, women will prove the most amenable to this photographer's eye. She must have put her subjects at ease, for in photographs of women at Fourth of July celebrations, or breaking horses, or sitting in front of their rough-hewn homes, they look at ease, unafraid to be themselves, wholly present to the camera. Their poses also speak of rapport, friendship with other women, and a keen sense of humor. These are qualities best designed to assure an enduring life in a tough place.

DECEMBER

In which Great Falls is born and bypassed, Ella Knowles becomes Montana's first woman lawyer, and Helen Clarke leaves Montana.

GREAT FALLS CITY
Located at the Great falls of the Missouri which furnish the
mightiest available Water-power on the American continent if
not on the globe, is the Queen City of the Northwest. . . . She is
destined by her natural resources and geographical position to
become the leading Manufacturing City between Minneapolis
and the Pacific, as well as the Railroad Center of Montana.

WHAT WOULD COMPEL A MAN, EVEN A TALL, STRONG engineer, to brave the worst of winter storms on a bitter cold night in the northern Rockies, all but alone save for a terrified Pend d'Oreille companion? What force, what cause would drive John Stevens over that pass at just over 5,000 feet on December 11, 1889? None other than the Great Northern and James Hill's search for the vector leading from the plains to the sea, from northcentral Montana to Seattle. Stevens' discovery of Marias Pass—really more of a re-discovery, since tribal people know the route—assures the newly named railroad can drive directly west from Bull Hook Bottoms (later named Havre) instead of diverting to Great Falls. As Hill explains to Paris Gibson in late December, "It would be folly to make a detour as far south as Great Falls and turn around and go north, using two sides of a triangle when one of them could be saved." Writing to a friend and key business partner, Hill prefers the

Paris Gibson. The History Museum, Great Falls, Montana

language of geometry to that of the heart. And so it is that Gibson discovers his beloved town, built largely through his vision, persistence, and partnerships, will not fall on the main line of the coming railway. Great Falls would now literally and figuratively be a sideline, a psychological and economic comedown for the rising town.

Great Falls was not even a glimmer in Gibson's eye when he migrated to Montana after failing at business in Minneapolis. He landed in Fort Benton on June 2, 1879, aboard the steamboat *Helena*, following the path of so many before him migrating from the upper Midwest to a Montana Territory that seemed ready for an economic takeoff. He was not a young man—he was 49 years old when he made the leap across the Dakota and Montana prairie. Montana had captured his imagination when he discovered fifteen to twenty thousand pounds of high-quality Montana wool during an inspection tour in Chicago. Gibson set to running sheep for mutton and wool, a reasonable proposition at a time when the open range lured so many with the promise of cattle kingdoms. Northern Montana apparently did not witness the conflict between sheep and cattle ranchers that would play out in dramatic fashion in Wyoming, and Gibson realized a solid income through the less glamorous livestock. No wonder he will observe in an autobiographical essay written late in life, "As I look back over the past 84 years, I can see plainly that my work on the farm and garden and in the timber woods and my enforced work in caring for our dumb animals during the long winter months has been of more value to me during my somewhat checkered life than the education afforded me in the academies of New England and at Bowdoin College, where I graduated in 1851." Gibson would remain a staunch advocate for the sheep industry throughout his life.

Paris Gibson's life changed in May, 1882, during a visit to the Great Falls of the Missouri, famous from the Lewis and Clark Expedition and visited often by newcomers to the region. A simple but powerful idea emerged in Gibson's mind as he tended sheep near the five cataracts forming "the Falls": He was staring at the only major dam site between Minneapolis and Spokane. A city built near that power source and linked to the copper kingdom of Butte and the range and grain lands of northcentral Montana could rival Minneapolis. Gibson turned to none other than Hill, a friend from his Minnesota days, for financial backing for the new town. Gibson offered a straightforward value proposition to the railroad titan: If he could extend his railroad to the prospective town on the upper Missouri before the Northern Pacific Railroad, he could claim a tidy profit. Gibson set forth his full, compelling appeal in a letter to Hill dated June 5, 1883:

> . . . a town at the mouth of [the] Sun River would have for its support and development, *1st* the gold and silver bearing lodes of the Belt Mountains, one of the richest if not the richest mineral belt of Montana. *2d* an available water power probably the greatest on this Continent, being in my opinion more than thirty times greater than the Falls of St. Anthony [at Minneapolis]. *3d* the most extensive stock ranges of Montana, the wool product especially being very large in this section. *4th* the most extensive coal deposit yet found in Montana, being distant not over five miles. *5th* An agricultural area comprising the eastern Sun River Valley, already occupied by farmers and stock growers from its source in the Mountains to its mouth— also all of the upper Teton and its tributaries also the rich slopes and valleys adjacent to the Belt Mountains, at least one hundred miles in length, which recent cultivation has demonstrated to be the best of wheat lands.

No wonder Hill made that journey to Montana in 1884 and fell under the spell of Gibson and Charles Broadwater. No wonder he drove himself and his workers mad with the push across

Dakota and eastern Montana the summer of 1887 to extend his
rail line from Minot to what would soon be Havre.

Meanwhile, Gibson set about platting his new city the summer of 1883, dreaming of a beautiful city. Great Falls is still
distinguished by the symmetry of its tree-lined streets and the
pastoral appeal of its aptly named Paris Gibson Park. More importantly for the town's economic future, Gibson, Broadwater,
Hill, and two other partners incorporated the Great Falls Water
Power and Townsite Company in 1887, with Hill controlling the
vast majority of the stock. Gibson struck a deal with the Lewisohn brothers from Butte that they would build a state-of-the-
art smelter to refine copper and zinc. In return, Gibson guaranteed construction of a dam at Black Eagle Falls, critical since the
new process of electrolytic refining central to the new smelter
would depend upon electricity generated by the dam. And so
the synergy of industrial refining processes and water power
would be fully realized in Gibson's new city. No wonder the
town's population expands from 800 in 1887 to nearly 4,000 by
1890. Completion of the Montana Central Line in 1889 enables
shipment of Butte copper and silver to Great Falls' new smelters
and refineries, and Black Eagle Falls Dam will be completed in
1890. Surely Great Falls will soon become a major rail center for
the Great Northern. What could possibly check this momentum
toward Gibson's city becoming truly a Montana Minneapolis?

And so the rude shock, the disappointment, the sense of
betrayal at the news late in 1889 that Hill would not route his
newly named railroad through the city created by a friend who
had assured him so much wealth, so much power in the new
state. Yet the Gibson-Hill partnership conforms so clearly to
the pattern set by the Higgins-Hammond relationship—the
older, place-bound man, focused on building local communities and realizing opportunities in Montana, would be bested
and even overwhelmed by a capitalist with far wider horizons
and far deeper pockets. Gibson will possess the self-awareness

to diagnose this power imbalance, for one of his major causes during his long, active political life will be to warn Montanans about the threat posed by eastern capital. He will come to fear the concentration of mining interests in fewer and fewer hands, threatening monopolistic control over the state (such as would be exhibited during Amalgamated Copper's shutdown of its operations for eighteen days in 1903 as it seeks to vanquish F. Augustus Heinze).

This commitment to local power also explains Gibson's persistent, some would say stubborn, defense of the 160-acre homestead. He will remain convinced, in the face of diehard counterarguments from many agriculturalists, that dryland farming on these small plots would support a robust population on the high plains and feed both the nation and his coffers. He is transfixed by the Jeffersonian dream of independent farmers occupying their own homesteads, building democratic communities and robust local economies. He will go so far as to oppose the Enlarged Homestead Act (increasing homesteads from 160 to 320 acres) during his six-year term as U. S. senator. Even visionaries have their blind spots.

"EXAMINED MISS KNOWLES FOR ADMISSION TO THE BAR AND was surprised to find her so well read. She beat all that I have ever examined." So writes Cornelius Hedges in his diary on Christmas Eve 1889, referring to his examination of Ella Knowles to become the first woman lawyer in Montana. Hedges, a prominent pioneer himself, had been joined by none other than Wilbur Fisk Sandersand the less-well-known but still important early Montanan John Clayberg. Knowles passes with flying colors, earning the surprised but sincere praise of at least one of her examiners. But it has not been easy for this brilliant young woman to reach this status, for she has had to clear several bars before being allowed to go before the elders to earn passage to a lawyer's title. She will go on to a full, complex, at times contro-

Ella Knowles Haskell. MONTANA HISTORICAL SOCIETY RESEARCH CENTER PHOTOGRAPH ARCHIVES, HELENA, MONTANA

versial career, but no one could deny her Hedge's praise or the honor of being first.

A child of New England, Knowles showed gumption early in life by insisting on an education at Bates College when few women were admitted. She excelled at her studies and at speech and debate. After graduating in 1884, she read law for three years, until poor health led a doctor to recommend removal to a drier, healthier climate for ailing lungs. Knowles chose Helena, perhaps because of a strong network of citizens with northeastern roots, including Sanders and Hedges. She quickly established herself as principal at a Helena school but must have felt called to the challenge, contest, and zest of the legal life, for she determined to pursue standing as an attorney in a territory that did not allow women to practice that profession. Not only could she call on the support of men with regional ties to her, but Knowles excelled at connecting with women through a variety of civic organizations, including the Theosophical Society, Daughters of the American Revolution, and Women's Relief Corps. She would prove skilled at converting this social capital into a legislative outcome that would allow her to take the bar exam during the Christmas season of 1889.

The Montana territorial legislature needed to pass a bill to grant women permission to serve as attorneys. The last legislature, called into session by Governor Leslie in January of 1889, debated with gusto the proposition that the legal profession would be open to members of both sexes. While the issue seemed to encourage as much teasing as serious reflection, legislators were inclined to follow suit. One issue cut both ways: Those deliberating the bill allowing women lawyers recognized that the measure mainly involved one charismatic individual, Ella Knowles. Her network had clearly done its work, bringing before the legislative body a bill that would transform her from assistant to attorney. The singularity of the proposition worked to Knowles' disadvantage in that legislators wondered why they should encode a substantial change to Montana law. On the other hand, if the bill effected the conversion of a lone woman to attorney rank, perhaps the law would not make all that much difference.

In the end the bill passed, and Knowles prepares for the exam that will mark her admission to the bar. But these signal victories are only preliminary steps on the path to stable, remunerative legal work. By her own account, written in 1907, "When I first began the practice of law, I was taken as a huge joke, and I could have sat in my office to this day and would not have had a case. But I didn't sit in the office; I went out and got my business to start with, and soon business came to me in abundance." She will tell with humor directed at herself and her male nemeses the story of her first effort to earn a living by collecting bills, a critical step in claiming her rights and status as lawyer. When virtually every male business owner refuses to put her services to use, she cajoles a store manager to give her the names of customers who have borrowed his umbrellas (an issue since he cannot go out on a rainy day), secures two of the missing devices from prominent citizens, and returns to the store demanding payment of $.50 for her effort. The store owner balks, upset Knowles has possibly alienated paying customers. However, the voice of the people prevails, for Knowles asks shoppers to affirm her rights, and when they assent, the store owner hands over two $.25 pieces. Knowles will claim she still has those two pieces when she composes her brief autobiography in 1907. They mark an important rite of passage.

Her first trial will involve a claim of $5 owed a Chinaman by a black store owner. Knowles will recall this initial courtroom effort as a severe test of her nerves, keeping her up at night to plot strategy. She wins the case when she proves through the use of a magnifying glass that the employer had indeed erased and altered the sum owed in his account book. This humble case will lead to many more in an illustrious legal career. She will

even run as the Populist Party's candidate for attorney general
in 1902, an office she seems to have sought at the suggestion of
others. To her credit, as with her persistence concerning college, the bar exam, and her first case, Knowles recognizes an
opportunity to elevate her profile and secure more clients. She
will travel the state stumping for the office, often impressing listeners with her oratorical skill committed to the Populist platform of silver coinage, women's rights, and overcoming income
inequality. Still, naysayers will persist. One reporter will mock
her New England accent, while the censorious Lizzie Fisk will
aver, "It was simply disgusting. She swung her arms and opened
her mouth and yelled. No other word expresses it." Whatever
doubts expressed by the squeamish Mrs. Fisk, and she may well
have been as put out by the Populist platform as the speaker's
style, Knowles will receive 11,465 votes, a substantial number,
more than those received by the Populist candidate for governor. The election winner, Henri Haskell, will be so impressed
by her campaigning that he asks her to serve as his Assistant
Attorney General. That office will lead to dramatic court cases
involving the likes of Marcus Daly and Paris Gibson, but also
matrimony to Haskell, though the marriage will end in divorce
when the husband chooses to relocate to Glendive.

Intelligent, charming, canny, and witty, Ella Knowles will
spend the last years of her life in Butte, working on mining cases
and acquiring property of her own. It's tempting to imagine this
keen, determined professional woman contesting the claims of
Amalgamated Mining, putting her Populist ideals to the service
of people subject to the whims of a powerful company. Though
she will die at the relatively young age of 50, her poor health at
last catching up with her, she will have made such a difference to
the status of women in her adopted state.

IT IS TIME FOR HELEN CLARKE TO LEAVE HER NATIVE STATE,
seek justice and reward in the wider world. She will reverse

the meaning of her Piegan name, Piotopowaka, "the Bird that Comes Home," taking her nephews to Carlisle Indian School in Pennsylvania, then seek work in the East, perhaps once again as an actress. Rumors reach her that the government needs allotment agents, and she might serve that cause if opportunity offers. Her poor mother, Coth-co-co-na, broken by her husband Malcolm's ghastly murder in 1869 at the hands of her relative, Owl Child, has just returned to the Blackfeet Reservation, close to her first home, and it is especially hard for Helen to abandon her. Yet all her striving for respect and belonging in Helena, in Montana, has failed utterly. Perhaps she is too headstrong, too "masculine," for the close-knit elites—perhaps it is simply that a woman of mixed white and Indian blood violates too many assumed principles of refinement, decency, and culture.

It was not easy returning to Montana in 1876 after that leap at notoriety on the New York stage. Though not the most gifted of thespians, Helen received encouraging reviews, observers commending her for her stature, bearing, and deep, strong, commanding voice. She loved being before an audience, playing a part (is she not always playing a part?), but an actress has to decide whether to give her all to the art, to give up everything for those moments of bliss on stage, and something prevented her surrendering to that calling.

So Helen returned to Montana, taking up teaching in Fort Benton, still a crude town for all its advances since she had last seen it. Wilbur Sanders, a godsend for people of outcast tribes and races, asked her to join him and his lovely family in Helena, to take on teaching at more affluent schools, to live in the comfort of a maturing town. How could Helen turn down such an opportunity? After all, Mr. Sanders had been such a good friend to her father, riding north to visit the ranch in Little Prickly Pear Canyon, often plying Malcolm for the good stories of the old times with the American Fur Company, sharing tall tales and cigars. How she admired the man's passionate defense of

Helen P. Clarke. Montana Historical Society Research Center Photograph Archives, Helena, Montana

people too often neglected or denied dignity. Many Montanans despised Mr. Sanders, calling him an obstructionist, a vulgar Republican, a Montana Mephistopheles. Yet how could he endure if he did not assert his rights, learned during that crucible of the Civil War and reinforced through the steady resistance of Democrats during these years after the war? He had to be hard, just as he was when he led the campaign against those road agents at Bannack and Virginia City in 1864. Yet what a kind man to Helen, a father, to be sure, and a wise counselor. It is her fondest hope he will be named one of Montana's first senators, a fitting cap to his distinguished life.

He and his loving wife encouraged Helen to run for the Superintendent of Instruction in Lewis and Clark County following her stint as a schoolteacher. He sensed her discontent in the pedagogical arts, feeling stifled and impatient at times. No wonder Helen repeated as a kind of chorus for her life, "Children should have nothing but the greatest admiration, the greatest respect, the greatest love and reverence for their teachers." However, she felt most foiled by parents who resisted her efforts at reform. Mrs. Robert Fisk, for one, made her opprobrium well known, withdrawing her children from Helen's classroom in a grand display of disdain. How ironic, given the natural political alliance between her hosts, the Sanders and Mr. Robert Fisk, editor of Helena's Republican newspaper. While Mrs. Fisk held up the fig leaf of disagreeing with Helen's teaching methods, her reference to her being a "breed" revealed her true motives. So many of these newcomers to the territory (and now state) had no knowledge of those earlier times when white men married Indian women, creating a race of children blending the two tribes. How fussy and dismissive so many of these refined ladies could be. And yet they too are of mixed nationality, mixed tribes, only they choose to conceal that truth beneath the title "American." Sometimes the refined ladies are little better than the poor white trash who trumpeted the superiority of their blood.

Helen often casts her mind back to her mother and father's early years in this region, how they were married at Fort Mackenzie at the mouth of the Marias River. Her father, called White Lodge Pole as a sign of respect, was loved, feared, and admired by the Blackfeet. No doubt Helen inherited his quick temper and occasional haughty pride, but also how he earned that pride through deed and character. The daughter remembers with special affection the words of General Sherman, upon discovering Malcolm's grave during his travels through Montana in 1877. The great man recalled her father as a fellow cadet at West Point and fondly summoned the bright, open-hearted, spirited young man who became a great factor for the American Fur Company. How Coth-co-co-na turned warm and thoughtful recalling their early married years. Visitors often misunderstood Helen's beautiful mother, who seemed so shy and reserved around strangers, but in truth she possessed a keen mind and deep insight into people. She often took her daughter aside to share her fears: How would Helen survive in the coming world, controlled by unfeeling newcomers, bringing with them beliefs and customs so alien to the Clarkes' home? How Helen wishes she could speak with her now, ask for her wisdom, her love, but her broken heart and mind create an impenetrable barrier between her soul and the world. Watching her tall, handsome, headstrong husband murdered on his own ranch wrenched the universe out of joint for Coth-co-co-na, and she never found a way to put it back in place.

So Helen must find her own way forward alone in these troubled, perplexing times, the age of tribes, when people fall in with their own races and assign others a place on the scale of humanity. What law is there in Montana for upholding an Indian's rights? Oh, she fully understands that her Indian kin must accept the new world of allotments, farming, boarding schools, and Christianity. Their old ways of tribal rites and hunting and camping wherever nature guided them can never come back.

The past has been foreclosed by the slaughter of the buffalo, the coming of the railroad, and the drive of so many Americans and foreigners into this country, not just to the Clarkes' home country on the Missouri but to loud towns such as Butte. Having served as the superintendent of all students in this fraught town of Helena, Helen realizes more than ever that the ways of the Americans are the only ways for the Indians. That is their only future. Perhaps she can find her destiny by helping the Indians enter that new world, perhaps she can ease their transition to a life of private property and self-respect through raising crops and families on their own land. Certainly Helen feels called to Carlisle, happy to bring her nephews by brother Horace to that impressive campus. Their leaders encourage her to serve as a role model for the young students, a woman of two tribes who has trod the world's most prestigious stages and guided an entire school district toward more progressive education. What a thrill it will be for her to reenact her favorite part from her stage years—the soothsaying gypsy in Walter Scott's *Guy Mannering*—recite favorite verses, take on a different role. Yes, she is very good at playing parts, and she can show these young people how to move forward through skill and grace.

Perhaps Helen will never return to Montana, a place of so many vexed emotions and confounding memories. Yet at night, as she drifts toward sleep, her mind may well repeat a chorus, a haunting chorus, one for which she has no ready reply: If not here, where? Where will she find home?

AFTER

In which Richard Littlebear describes a Cheyenne homecoming and Joseph Kinsey Howard reflects on Montanans' good fortune.

A Conversation with Grandma
(excerpt)

Neȯhkėsaaȧevesee 'kotsenovahe naa ovahe tseȯhkeevėheto,

naohkėsoȧamemȧxaȧooȧe tsetȧhaȧešėstanoveto.

You were not the hugging kind, but you've touched me all of my life.

Naȅstse neestsestȯtse tsehešemȧxaȧoeto, nasoȧheneȧena:

One way you touched me I remember:

Hoȧeešema 'seoȧenemenatse, neokeevȧhohpoȧanenemane

When we took down our camps from berry-picking time every fall

neohkeevȧhoohtoȧeohtsemane,

and as we rode home on the horse-drawn wagon,

nestaohkeevȧhootoo'o, hoehase
nestaohkeevȧhotoove'hoohtanȯtse hene

tsehae'eho'omenaa'ëstse hoehase.

you would look back to the mountains.

Nestaohkeveše:"Ve'kesȯhnestoohe!

You would call me by my Cheyenne name: Howling Bird,

Nexhooseve'hahtsėstse.

Come home with us.

—RICHARD LITTLEBEAR VE'KESOHNESTOOHE

The sunset holds infinite promise. Fire sweeps up from behind the Rockies to consume the universe, kindles the whole horizon, and all the great sky is flame; then suddenly it falters and fades atop the distant peaks and the lonely buttes, ebbs and is lost in secret coulees. The Montanan is both humbled and exalted by this blazing glory filling his world, yet so quickly dead; he cannot but marvel that such a puny creature as he should be privileged to stand there, unharmed, and watch.

—JOSEPH KINSEY HOWARD

SOURCES

*All verbatim excerpts have been indicated in the text
by quotation marks or block quotations.*

INTRODUCTION

9   *In its present form* Roosevelt, 24.

10   *We were really white Indians* Abbott, 16.

VISIONS

15   *I have not told* Linderman, *Plenty-coups,* 311.

16   *The reservation system* Morgan, 3-4.

17   *Montana has undoubtedly* Brisbin, 83-84.

18   *[W]e have a country* Martin, 332.

19   *The adoption of the [Montana State] Constitution* Spence, 306.

20   *Linderman later reported* Linderman, 44.

JANUARY

21   *With its mines of wealth* Butte Daily Miner, January 1, 1889.

21   *Young Man Afraid of His Horses dictates* Information drawn
     from Rzechzkowski and Hoxie, *Parading through History.* For
     further discussion of tribal rapport across apparent lines of
     conflict, see Thompson, Kootenai Culture Committee, and
     Pikunni Traditional Association.

21-22 *I want to visit the Crows* Rzechzkowski, 2.

23   *[h]e was old and undersized* Alderson, 92-93.

24   *In the summer season* Cowen, 233.

24   *See how the white men* Hoxie, *Parading through History,* 149.

25   *On the 6th day of the first month* Information on Daly drawn
     from Emmons, Glasscock, Malone, Spence, and Toole, "The
     Genesis of the Clark-Daly Feud."

25   *to tell you the truth* Malone, *Battle for Butte*, 88.

30   *The conspiracy was a gigantic one* Spence, 175-76. Clark
     shared these sharp opinions in a letter to Martin Maginnis,
     Democratic stalwart, dated November 10, 1888.

32   *At this crisis in our history* Leslie, 1.

34   *It is almost twenty-five years* Leslie, 18.

FEBRUARY

37   *Alderman Bullard returned yesterday* Daily Yellowstone Journal,
     February 2, 1889.

37-38 *SIR: I am in the painful condition* Harrison, 3. Information on
     Louis Riel, the Métis, and the Landless Indians drawn from
     Burt, Howard, *Strange Empire*, River, Siggins, and Vrooman.

42   *The work was monotonous* Schoeberg, 82.

43   *Mr. Riel says* Sun River Sun, June 12, 1884.

45-46 *That the Hudson's Bay Company* Harrison, 7.

46   *I used to live wretchedly* Siggins, 401.

47   *Soon after the Riel rebellion* Helena Independent, January 1,
     1889.

48   *We have in Northern and Western Montana, Fort Benton River
     Press*, June 26, 1889.

49   *As I entered the cabin, The Philipsburg Mail*, February 14,
     1889. Information on the Chinese in Montana extracted from
     Flaherty, Merritt, and Swartout.

50   *insurmountable barrier* Swartout, 103.

51   *"verily the road"* Livingston Daily Enterprise, June 10, 1884.

51   *The Chinaman's life* Swartout, 113.

52   *Down with Chinese Cheap Labor* Flaherty, 393.

52   *Dr. Huie Pock. 12 Years* Butte Inter Mountain, June 1, 1889.

54   *That by the concerted* Pock and Loy, 1-2.

56 *In Miles City the Knights* Information on the Knights of Pythias and other fraternal orders drawn from Emmons, "The Socialization of Uncertainty," and Schmidt.

56 *We are proud* Daily Yellowstone Journal, February 21, 1889.

58 *The copper mining city of Butte* Emmons, "The Socialization of Uncertainty," 147.

MARCH

61 *Cattle bands are constantly growing* Fergus County Argus, March 21, 1889.

61 *Charlie Russell turns 25* Information on Charlie Russell drawn from Dippie, Nancy Russell, and Taliaferro.

61-62 *I have tirde [tried]* Dippie, 9.

64-65 *Speakin' of cowpunchers* Charles M. Russell, 1.

65 *Who better to re-see* Information on Bower is drawn from Engen and Lamont.

65 *My father taught me music* Engen, 48.

68 *In northern Montana* Bower, 1.

69 *Of a truth, [Val] was different* Bower, 210.

69 *There was an old* Alderson, 221.

70, 72 *The writer has just* Montana Memory Project. For information on the Métis in the Lewistown area in the 1880s, see Harroun Foster.

73-74 *Our Children being* Horne, 184.

74 *Madame fails less* Horne, 182.

74 *Friends—the dead wife* Horne, 186.

APRIL

75 *Seven car loads of passengers* New North-west, April 5, 1889.

75 *The beginning of the American republic* New North-west, April 26, 1889.

75   *On the first day of the fourth month* Information on Roosevelt
      and the myth of the West drawn from Di Silvestro, Slotkin, and
      Trachtenberg.

77   *Rich men's sons* Abbott, 191.

77   *A true 'cow town'* Roosevelt, 7.

79   *While the slaughter* Di Silvestro, 116-17.

80   *The best days of ranching* Roosevelt, 24.

81   *The peculiarity of American institutions* Turner, 2.

81   *The club erected* Hoxie, *A Final Promise*, 84.

82-83 *The early days of the reservation* Stands in Timber, 419-20.

83   *Montana's most voluble storyteller* Information on Garcia
      gathered from Smith, Stein, and Mabel C. Olson.

83   *All of my associates* Garcia, 364.

86   *He knew that after leaving* Garcia, xvi.

MAY

89   *Eph. Harrison and Ccl. Scheetz* Helena Weekly Herald, May 2,
      1889.

89   *Responsible parties just in from* Helena Weekly Herald, May 9,
      1889.

89   *She moves with fierce force* Information on Mary Gleim and
      prostitution in early Montana gathered from Baumler, "Devil's
      Perch," Foley, and Petrik.

90   *These women were great spenders* Gordon, "Gone Are the
      Days," 10.

91   *Mary Gleim, who was convicted* Anaconda Standard,
      September 15, 1894.

91   *Mother Gleim broke loose* The New North-west, February 14,
      1896.

91-92 *Mary Gleim is dead* Daily Missoulian, February 23, 1914.

93   *In a world of horses* Information on Spokane's victory gathered
      from the *Helena Independent Record* May 10, 1889 and June 26,

1889, Melin-Moser, the *Missoulian* May 2, 2015, and the online *Racing Forum.*

95 *the raw-boned brute* *Missoulian*, May 2, 2015.

96-97 *Petition to the President* The headline and subsequent quotations are from *The Daily Yellowstone Journal*, May 28, 1889. Information on the controversy over the Northern Cheyenne Reservation is drawn from *We, the Northern Cheyenne People*, Greene, Grinnell, and Svingen.

97 *We have come to ask* *We the Northern Cheyenne People*, 26.

100-101 *Of about 150 Cheyennes* Grinnell, *The Fighting Cheyennes*, 426.

101-102 *In regard to the proposed removal* Svingen, 169-70.

JUNE

103 *Mr. John J. Kennedy of this city* *Great Falls Tribune*, June 5, 1889.

103 *Granville Stuart is in love* Information on Granville and Belle Stuart gathered from Hakola, Milner and O'Connor, and Abbott.

103-104 *Being an Indian* Abbott, 190.

105 *And now let the birds* Milner and O'Connor, 273.

105 *I know twenty* Milner and O'Connor, 278.

106 *The teacher is the girl* Milner and O'Connor, 278-79.

106 *It is awful to think* Milner and O'Connor, 137.

107 *Went down the river* Stuart, volume 1, 122.

108 *If we can obtain* Hakola, 233.

110 *From the Porcupine* Stuart, volume 1, 104.

110 *Left Miles City* Stuart, volume 1, 105.

110-111 *there appeared a most interesting* Kelly, xi-xii.

111 *Huffman is one* Stuart, volume 1, 111-12.

112 *Granville himself is all right* Hakola, 251.

112 *Who wouldn't pick it* Information on the founding of Havre drawn from *Grits, Guts, and Gusto* and Jenks.

115 *I saw the last Sun Dance* Stands in Timber, 480.

JULY

117 *At noon to-day a deliberative body* Helena Independent, July 4, 1889.

117 *Rudyard Kipling, 23, pauses* Information on Kipling extracted from Arrell Gibson and Jones.

118 *Livingston is a town* Gibson, 81-82.

119 *A picturesque old man* Gibson, 83.

119 *To-day I am* Gibson, 85.

120 *the great American nation* Gibson, 150.

120 *Clara McAdow greets* Information on Clara and Perry "Bud" McAdow drawn from Van West, an unpublished manuscript in the Montana Historical Society circular file, and multiple newspaper sources.

125 *the biggest mine* Fergus County Argus, March 28, 1889.

127 *Lizzie Fisk writes* Information on Lizzie Fisk drawn from Petrik and Meyers.

129 *Like you, I wonder how ladies find time* Meyers, 132.

132 *To assist working women* Helena Weekly Herald, June 16, 1887.

133 *I do not intend sending* Meyers, 107.

135 *He is one of the new men* Information on Wibaux, Roosevelt, and De Mores gathered from Di Silvestro and Welsh. For a full treatment of the emerging cattle industry in late-nineteenth-century Montana, see Michael M. Miller.

137 *In other words it is a funny life* Welsh, 34.

138, 140 *Medora had a short season* Daily Yellowstone Journal, February 6, 1889.

140 *Samuel Hauser, Montana magnate* Information about Hauser extracted from Chadwick, Clinch, Gordon, Hakola, Linderman, Malone, Roeder, and Lang, and Robbins.

140 *I feel it is just* Robbins,108.

141 *Sitting by our fire* Linderman, 76.

143 *I will state to you* Clinch, 97.

144 *The principal supporting business* Hugo, 216.

AUGUST

147   *The United States senate committee* Livingston Enterprise, August 3, 1889.

147   *The one-armed autodidact* Information on Powell gathered from Reisner, Rowland, Stegner, and Worster.

150   *in the western half of America* Proceedings, 820.

150-151 *The whole area of Montana* Proceedings, 822.

152   *The Ghost Dance comes* Information on the Ghost Dance at Fort Belknap, as well as information about the Aaniiih and Assiniboine adaptations to the reservation, is drawn from Lesser and Fowler.

152   *When the sun died* Greene, 68.

153   *The past season has been* Simons, 231.

153   *The old people are fast wedded* Simons, 232.

154   *This fasting was in connection* Stands in Timber, 61.

154   *The agent to the Crow reservation* Information about Sword Bearer's rebellion is drawn from Calloway, Hoxie, *Parading through History,* Lear, and Rzechzkowski.

156   *He is greatly improved* Wyman, 226.

158   *The dream of Plenty-coups* Linderman, *Plenty-coups,* 73.

159   *A Helena titan's dream* Information on Broadwater drawn from Birkby, Lang, Malone, *James J. Hill,* and Paladin and Baucus.

159   *a lofty and picturesque structure* Birkby, 62.

161   *I cannot forget* Malone, *James J. Hill*, 116.

162   *COLONEL BROADWATER DEAD* Helena Independent, May 25, 1892.

163   *It was late summer* Alderson, 192.

166   *When you live so close* Alderson, 171.

166   *Few families living* Alderson, 73.

167   *An Indian sub-chief* Alderson, 101-02.

169   *[Chief Black Wolf] must have* Stands in Timber, 78-79.

171   *The papooses [her children] did not* Alderson, 189.

171   *After my husband's death* Alderson, 263.

SEPTEMBER

173   *For some time past* Butte Semi-Weekly Miner, September 25, 1889.

173   *The retiring Indian agent at Fort Peck* Information on the Fort Peck Reservation gathered from Cowen and Miller, et al.

174   *are mixed blood; 610 wear citizens' dress wholly* Cowen, 233. All other excerpts taken from this source.

176   *An African American child* Information on Rose Gordon drawn from Foley and Sherfy Walter and Johnson.

176   *It gives me great pleasure* Gordon, "My School Days." All further school memories from this source.

178   *I must tell you about the thrill* Meagher County News, February 5, 1964.

179   *I have just heard* Johnson, 97.

179   *A visit between two men* Information on Mad Wolf, Grinnell, the Sweetgrass Treaty, and the Dawes Act gathered from Farr, Harper, Hoxie, *A Final Promise,* McClintock, Murray, Punke, and Sherry Smith, "George Bird Grinnell."

179   *You are good. . .* Farr, 70.

182   *The Blackfeet people* Murray, 1.

183   *I am not an Eastern sentimentalist* Grinnell, "He Ought to Be Removed"; all subsequent Grinnell quotations from this source.

186-187 *One afternoon in midsummer* McClintock, 26.

187   *The Great Northern Railway is born* Information on Hill is drawn from Howard, *Montana, High, Wide, and Handsome,* Malone, *James J. Hill,* and Martin.

190   *Thus was the stage set* Howard, *Montana, High, Wide, and Handsome,* 172.

191   *Could you spot a financial and mining genius* Information on Heinze assembled from Glassock, Howard, *Montana, High, Wide, and Handsome,* McNellis, Malone, *Battle for Butte,* Malone, Roeder, and Lang, and Swibold.

194   *How did you deal* Toole, *Montana,* 202.

196   *These people are my enemies* Howard, *Montana, High, Wide, and Handsome,* 78.

196   *A blackmailer, a thief* Swibold, 76.

197   *No one human being* McNellis, 136.

OCTOBER

199   *The grand jury at its recent session* *Philipsburg Mail,* October 17, 1889.

199   *Can you imagine it* Information on Sarah Bickford acquired from Baumler, "Sarah Gammon Bickford," Queen-Lacey and Peterson and Svingen.

203   *They move into their new home* Information on the Abbotts drawn from Milner and O'Connor.

203   *Ted, there's a pair of us* Abbott, 145.

203   *my spur catched* Abbott, 81.

207   *They wanted us* Abbott, 207.

207   *After we were married* Abbott, 208.

207   *It is the least they can do* Information on Hammond and Higgins gleaned from Greg Gordon and Mathews.

209   *Yesterday Missoula was the scene* *Daily Missoulian,* October 17, 1889.

NOVEMBER

215   *Deep down in the gloomy depths* *Butte Semi-Weekly Miner,* November 27, 1889.

215   *Let this be the day* Information on Charlo's fateful decision is drawn from Ferguson, "Mary Ann Pierre Topsseh Coombs," Mary Ronan, Peter Ronan, and Walter.

215   *I will go* Walter, 64.

217   *The outlook for the Indians* Peter Ronan, 229.

218   *Owing to the prejudices* Peter Ronan, 230.

218   *You may carry me* Walter, 59.

219   *everyone was in tears* Ferguson, "Mary Ann Pierre Topsseh Coombs," 103.

219   *That the announcement of realized statehood* Anaconda *Standard*, November 9, 1889. Information on Montana's first legislature gathered from Malone, Roeder, and Lang and Spence.

225   *The Standard was the first newspaper* Anaconda *Standard*, January 15, 1890.

226   *The robbery of Montana was completed* Anaconda *Standard*, April 17, 1890.

226   *Frank Linderman believes the old trapper* Information on Linderman culled from Merriam, River, and Sherry Smith, "Reimagining the Indian."

228   *I had had the bad luck* Linderman, 5.

228   *Sometimes, especially in damp weather* Linderman, 92.

229   *My literary efforts had failed* Linderman, 170.

230   *Claiming kinship with the Crees* Linderman, 141.

230   *How well I remember my first meeting* River, 51.

231   *The white man is the natural enemy* Sherry Smith, "Reimagining," 154-55.

231   *A young woman sits sidesaddle* Information about Cameron is drawn from Lucey, Raban, Hager, and Roberts and Wordsworth. For a full discussion of British ex-pats in the western United States, see Rico.

234   *Apart from the pleasant emotions* Raban, 72.

DECEMBER

237   *GREAT FALLS CITY Located at the* Great Falls Leader, December 1, 1889.

237   *What would compel a man* Information on Gibson and Stevens gathered from Paris Gibson, Malone, *James J. Hill*, Roeder, "A Settlement on the Plains," and White.

237   *It would be folly* Malone, *James J. Hill*, 132.

239   *As I look back* Gibson, 2.

240 *A town at the mouth* White, 62-63.

242 *Examined Miss Knowles* Roeder, "Crossing the Gender Line,"
64. Information on Knowles gathered from this source.

245 *When I first began* Anaconda Standard, February 3, 1907.

246 *It was simply disgusting* Roeder, "Crossing the Gender Line,"
71.

246 *It is time for Helen Clarke* Information on Helen Clarke has
been drawn from Ferguson, "Helena Piotopowaka Clarke," "A
Sketch," the Clarke Papers, and Graybill.

249 *Children should have nothing* Helen Clarke Papers. Reprinted
by permission of the Montana Historical Society.

Note: After serving as an allotment agent in Oklahoma, Clarke will
return to Montana to settle on the Blackfeet Reservation with
her brother Horace. There she will establish a kind of literary
salon; she will also become host to many visitors who wish
to experience and know the American Indian through her.
Perhaps most surprisingly, she will serve as a guide and comfort
for the Blackfeet people, hoping to ease their transition to a life
so different from that of their ancestors.

AFTER

252-253 "A Conversation with My Grandmother," *Birthright*, 57. This
passage is used by permission from Dr. Littlebear.

253 *The sunset holds infinite promise* Howard, *Montana, High,
Wide, and Handsome*, 328.

REFERENCES

Books, Articles, and Documents

Abbott, E. C. ("Teddy Blue"), and Helena Huntington Smith. *We Pointed Them North: Recollections of a Cowpuncher.* Ca. 1939. Reprint Norman: University of Oklahoma Press, 1955.

Alderson, Nannie, with Helena Huntington Smith. *A Bride Goes West.* Ca. 1942. Reprint Lincoln: University of Nebraska Press, 1969.

Baumler, Ellen. "Devil's Perch: Prostitution from Suite to Cellar in Butte, Montana." *Montana The Magazine of Western History* 48, 3 (Autumn, 1998): 4-21.

_____. "Sarah Gammon Bickford: From Slave to Businesswoman." In *Beyond Schoolmarms and Madams: Montana Women's Stories.* Ed. Martha Kohl. Helena: Montana Historical Society Press, 2016. Pp. 218-221.

Birkby, Jeff. *Touring Hot Springs: Montana and Wyoming.* Guilford, CT: Morris, 2013.

Birthright: Born to Poetry—A Collection of Montana Indian Poetry. Helena: Montana Office of Public Instruction, 2012.

Bower, B. M. *Lonesome Land.* Ca. 1912. Reprint Lincoln: University of Nebraska Press, 1997.

Brisbin, James S. *The Beef Bonanza; or, How to Get Rich on the Plains.* Ca. 1881. Reprint Norman: University of Oklahoma Press, 1959.

Burt, Larry. "Nowhere Left to Go: Montana's Crees, Métis, and Chippewas and the Creation of Rocky Boy's Reservation." *Great Plains Quarterly* 7, 3 (Summer, 1987): 195-209.

Calloway, Colin. "Sword Bearer and the 'Crow Outbreak' of 1887." *Montana The Magazine of Western History,* 36, 4 (Autumn, 1986): 38-51.

Chadwick, Robert A. "Montana's Silver Mining Era: Great Boom and Great Bust." *Montana The Magazine of Western History,* 32, 2 (Spring, 1982): 16-31.

Clarke, Helen P. "A Sketch of Malcolm Clarke, A Corporate Member of the Historical Society of Montana." *Contributions to the Historical Society of Montana,* Vol. 2. Helena: State Publishing Company, 1896. Pp. 255-68.

Clinch, Thomas A. *Urban Populism and Free Silver in Montana.* Missoula: University of Montana Press, 1970.

Cowen, D. O. "Report of Fort Peck Agency." *Annual report of the commissioner of Indian affairs, for the year 1889.* Pp. 232-34.

Dippie, Brian W., ed. "Introduction." In *Charlie Russell Roundup: Essays on America's Favorite Cowboy Artist.* Helena: Montana Historical Society Press, 1999. Pp. 1-32.

Di Silvestro, Roger L. *Theodore Roosevelt in the Badlands: A Young Politician's Quest for Recovery in the American West.* New York: Walker and Company, 2011.

Emmons, David M. *Beyond the American Pale: The Irish in the West, 1845-1910.* Norman: University of Oklahoma Press, 2010.

_____. "The Orange and the Green in Montana: A Reconsideration of the Clark-Daly Feud." In *The Montana Heritage: An Anthology of Historical Essays.* Ed. Robert R. Swartout Jr. and Harry W. Fritz. Helena: Montana Historical Society Press, 1992. Pp. 149-70.

_____. "The Socialization of Uncertainty: The Ancient Order of Hibernians in Butte, Montana 1880-1925." In *Montana: A Cultural Medley.* Ed. Robert R. Swartout Jr. Helena: Farcountry, 2015. Pp. 146-175.

Engen, Orrin A. *Writer of the Plains: A Biography of B. M. Bower.* Culver City: Pontine, 1973.

Farr, William E. "A Point of Entry: The Blackfeet Adoption of Walter McClintock." In *Lanterns on the Prairie: The Blackfeet*

Photographs of Walter McClintock. Ed. Steven L.Grafe. Norman: University of Oklahoma Press, 2009. Pp. 43-81.

Ferguson, Laura. "Helen Piotopowaka Clarke and the Persistence of Prejudice." In *Beyond Schoolmarms and Madams: Montana Women's Stories.* Ed. Martha Kohl. Helena: Montana Historical Society Press, 2016. Pp. 171-73.

_____. "Mary Ann Pierre Topsseh Coombs and the Bitterroot Salish." In *Beyond Schoolmarms and Madams.* Pp. 101-04.

Flaherty, Stacey A. "Boycott in Butte: Organized Labor and the Chinese Community, 1896-1897." In *Chinese on the American Frontier.* Ed. Arif Dirlik. Lanham: Rowan and Littlefield, 2001. Pp. 393-413.

Foley, Jodie. "Missoula's Murderous Madam: The Life of Mary Gleim." In *Speaking Ill of the Dead: Jerks in Montana History.* Ed. Dave Walter. Helena: TwoDot, 2000. Pp. 85-98.

_____ and Marcella Sherfy Walter. "Rose Gordon: Daughter of a Slave and Small-Town Activist." In *Beyond Schoolmarms and Madams: Montana Women's Stories.* Ed. Martha Kohl. Helena: Montana Historical Society Press, 2016. Pp. 20-22.

Fowler, Loretta. *Shared Symbols, Contested Meanings: Gros Ventre Culture and History, 1778-1984.* Ithaca: Cornell University Press, 1987.

Gibson, Arrell Morgan, ed. *American Notes: Rudyard Kipling's West.* Norman: University of Oklahoma Press, 1981.

Gibson, Paris. Autobiographical manuscript. The History Museum, Great Falls.

Glasscock, C. B. *The War of the Copper Kings, Greed, Power, and Politics: The Billion-Dollar Battle for Butte, Montana, the Richest Hill on Earth.* Ca.1935. Reprint Helena: Riverbend Publishing, 2002.

Gordon, Greg. *When Money Grew on Trees: A. B. Hammond and the Age of the Timber Baron.* Norman: University of Oklahoma Press, 2014.

Gordon, Rose. "Gone Are the Days." Unpublished memoir. Emmanuel Taylor Gordon Papers, Montana Historical Society Archives, MC 150.

_____. "My School Days." Unpublished memoir. Emmanuel Taylor Gordon Papers, Montana Historical Society Archives, MC 150.

Graybill, Andrew R. *The Red and the White: A Family Saga of the American West*. New York: Norton, 2013.

Greene, Jerome A. *American Carnage: Wounded Knee, 1890*. Norman: University of Oklahoma Press, 2014.

Grinnell, George Bird. *The Fighting Cheyennes*. Ca. 1915. Reprint Norman: University of Oklahoma Press, 1955.

_____. "He Ought to Be Removed: An Indian Agent's Many Misdeeds." *New York Times,* March 4, 1889.

Grits, Guts, and Gusto. Havre: Hill County Bicentennial Commission, 1976.

Hager, Kristi. *Evelyn Cameron: Montana's Frontier Photographer*. Helena: Farcountry, 2007.

Hakola, John William. "Samuel T. Hauser and the Economic Development of Montana: A Case Study in Nineteenth-Century Frontier Capitalism." Dissertation, Indiana University, 1961.

Harper, Andrew C. "Conceiving Nature: The Creation of Montana's Glacier National Park." *Montana The Magazine of Western History* 60, 2 (Summer, 2010): 3-24.

Harrison, Benjamin. "Message from the President of the United States, Transmitting, in response to the Senate resolution of February 11, 1889, a report upon the case of Louis Riel." March 19, 1889.

Harroun Foster, Martha. "'Just Following the Buffalo': Origins of a Montana Métis Community." In *Montana: A Cultural Medley*. Ed. Robert R. Swartout Jr. Helena: Farcountry, 2015. Pp. 55-93.

Helen Clarke Papers. Montana Historical Society Archives. SC1153.

Horne, Robert Milton. "James Fergus—Frontier Businessman, Miner, Rancher, Free Thinker." Dissertation, University of Montana, 1971.

Howard, Joseph Kinsey. *Montana, High, Wide, and Handsome.* New Haven: Yale University Press, 1943.

_____. *Strange Empire: A Narrative of the Northwest.* Ca.1952. Reprint St. Paul: Minnesota Historical Society Press, 1994.

Hoxie, Frederick E. *A Final Promise: The Campaign to Assimilate the Indians, 1880-1920.* Ca. 1984. Reprint Lincoln: University of Nebraska Press, 2001.

_____. *Parading through History: The Making of the Crow Nation in America, 1805-1935.* New York: Cambridge University Press, 1995.

Hugo, Richard. *Making Certain It Goes On: The Collected Poems of Richard Hugo.* New York: Norton, 1984.

Jenks, Jim. "Historic and Architecturally Significant Resources of Downtown Havre, Montana, 1889-1959." National Register of Historic Places Continuation Sheet.

Johnson, Michael K. *Hoo-Doo Cowboys and Bronze Buckaroos: Conceptions of the African-American West.* Oxford: University Press of Mississippi, 2014.

Jones, Langdon Y. "At Large in the West." *Montana The Magazine of Western History* 64, 3 (Autumn, 2014): 24-35.

Kelly, Luther S. *"Yellowstone Kelly": The Memoirs of Luther S. Kelly.* Ed. M. M. Quaife. Ca. 1926. Repint Lincoln: University of Nebraska Press, 1973.

Lamont, Victoria. *Westerns: A Women's History.* Lincoln: University of Nebraska Press, 2016.

Lang, William L. "Charles A. Broadwater and the Main Chance in Montana." *Montana The Magazine of Western History,* 39, 3 (Summer, 1989): 30-36.

Lear, Jonathan. *Radical Hope: Ethics in the Face of Cultural Devastation.* Cambridge: Harvard University Press, 2006.

Leslie, Preston H. "Governor's Message." Helena: no printer, 1889.

Lesser, Alexander. *The Pawnee Ghost Dance Hand Game: Ghost Dance Revival and Ethnic Identity.* Ca.1978. Reprint Lincoln: University of Nebraska Press, 1996.

Linderman, Frank B. *Montana Adventure: The Recollections of Frank B. Linderman.* Ed. H. G. Merriam. Lincoln: University of Nebraska Press, 1968.

_____. *Plenty-coups, Chief of the Crows.* Ca. 1930. Reprint Lincoln: University of Nebraska Press, 1962.

Lucey, Donna M. *Photographing Montana, 1894-1928: The Life and Work of Evelyn Cameron.* Ca. 1990. Reprint Missoula: Mountain Press Publishing, 2001.

McClintock, Walter. *The Old North Trail: Life, Legends and Religion of the Blackfeet Indians.* Ca. 1910. Reprint Lincoln: University of Nebraska Press, 1992.

McNelis, Sarah. *Copper King at War: The Biography of F. Augustus Heinze.* Missoula: University of Montana Press, 1968.

Malone, Michael P. *Battle for Butte: Mining and Politics on the Northern Frontier, 1864-1906.* Seattle: University of Washington Press, 1981.

_____. *James J. Hill: Empire Builder of the Northwest.* Norman: University of Oklahoma Press, 1996.

_____, Richard B. Roeder, and William L. Lang. *Montana: A History of Two Centuries.* Revised edition. Seattle: University of Washington Press, 1991.

Martin, Albro. *James J. Hill and the Opening of the Northwest.* St. Paul: Minnesota Historical Society Press, 1991.

Mathews, Allan James. *A Guide to Historic Missoula.* Helena: Montana Historical Society Press, 2002.

Melin-Moser, Catharine. "In the Winner's Circle: How Montana Thoroughbreds Upset the Nineteenth Century's Racing Establishment." *Montana The Magazine of Western History* 64, 4 (Winter, 2014): 23-41.

Merriam, H. G. "The Life and Work of Frank B. Linderman." In Frank B. Linderman, *Montana Adventure: The Recollections of*

Frank B. Linderman. Ed. H. G. Merriam. Lincoln: University of Nebraska Press, 1968. Pp. 199-214.

Merritt, Christopher William. "'The Coming Man from Canton': Chinese Experience in Montana (1862-1943)." Dissertation, University of Montana, 2010.

Meyers, Rex C., ed. *Lizzie: The Letters of Elizabeth Chester Fisk, 1864-1893.* Missoula: Mountain Press Publishing, 1989.

Miller, David R., et al. *The History of the Fort Peck Assiniboine and Sioux Tribes, 1800-2000.* Poplar: Fort Peck Community College, 2008.

Miller, Michael M. "Cowboys and Capitalists: The XIT Ranch in Texas and Montana, 1885-1912." *Montana The Magazine of Western History* 65, 4 (Winter, 2015): 3-28.

Milner, Clyde A., II, and Carol A. O'Connor. *As Big as the West: The Pioneer Life of Granville Stuart.* New York: Oxford University Press, 2009.

Morgan, T. J. "Commissioner's Report." *Annual report of the commissioner of Indian affairs, for the year 1889.* Pp. 3-91.

Murray, Carol. *The Days of the Blackfeet: A Historical Overview of the Blackfeet Indians for K-12 Teachers in Montana.* Browning: Blackfeet Community College, 2008.

Olson, Mabel C. Montana Writers Project Interview with Andrew Garcia, July 26-August 1, 1940. MC376, Folder 8/7, Montana Historical Society Archives.

Paladin, Vivian, and Jean Baucus. *Helena: An Illustrated History.* Helena: Lewis and Clark Historical Society, 1983.

Peterson, Bill, and Orlan Svingen. "Finding Sarah Gammon Bickford." http://www.sarahbickford.org/story.html Accessed May 14, 2016.

Petrik, Paula. *No Step Backward: Women and Family on the Rocky Mountain Mining Frontier, Helena, Montana, 1865-1900.* Helena: Montana Historical Society Press, 1987.

Pock, Huie, and Quon Loy. Affadavit in the Circuit Court of the United States, Ninth Circuit, District of Montana, April 15, 1897.

Proceedings and Debates of the Constitutional Convention Held in the City of Helena, Montana July 4th, 1889, August 17th, 1889. Helena: State Publishing Company, 1921.

Punke, Michael. *Last Stand: George Bird Grinnell, the Battle to Save the Buffalo, and the Birth of the New West.* New York: Smithsonian, 2007.

Queen-Lacey, Marlette C. *From Slave to Water Magnate.* New York: IUniverse, 2006.

Raban, Jonathan. *Bad Land: An American Romance.* New York: Pantheon, 1996.

Racing Forum Online. "Spokane, the Kentucky Derby winner of 1889, a part of Montana folklore." Accessed May 23, 2016.

Reisner, Marc. *Cadillac Desert: The American West and Its Disappearing Water.* New York: Penguin, 1986.

Rico, Monica. *Nature's Noblemen: Transatlantic Masculinities and the Nineteenth-Century American West.* New Haven: Yale University Press, 2013.

River, Celeste. "Mountain in His Memory: Frank Bird Linderman, His Role in Acquiring the Rocky Boy Indian Reservation for the Montana Chippewa and Cree, and the Importance of that Experience in the Development of His Literary Career." Master's Thesis, University of Montana, 1990.

Robbins, William G. *Colony and Empire: The Capitalist Transformation of the American West.* Lawrence: University Press of Kansas, 1994.

Roberts, Ann, and Christine Wordsworth. "Divas, Divorce and Disclosure: Hidden Narratives in the Diaries of Evelyn Cameron." *Montana The Magazine of Western History* 64, 2 (Summer, 2014): 46-62.

Roeder, Richard B. "Crossing the Gender Line: Ella L. Knowles, Montana's First Woman Lawyer." *Montana The Magazine of Western History* 32, 3 (Summer, 1982): 64-75.

_____. "A Settlement on the Plains: Paris Gibson and the Building of Great Falls." *Montana The Magazine of Western History* 42, 4 (Autumn, 1992): 4-19.

Ronan, Peter. "Report of Flathead Agency." *Annual report of the commissioner of Indian affairs, for the year 1889.* Pp. 227-31.

Roosevelt, Theodore. *Ranch Life and the Hunting Trail.* Ca. 1888. New York: Century, 1911.

Rowland, Russell. *Fifty-Six Counties: A Montana Journey.* Bozeman: Bangtail Press, 2016.

Russell, Charles M. *Trails Plowed Under: Stories of the Old West.* Ca. 1927. Reprint Lincoln: University of Nebraska Press, 1996.

Russell, Nancy Cooper. "My Charlie." *Montana The Magazine of Western History* 8, 3(Fall, 1958): 81-89.

Rzechzkowski, Frank. *Uniting the Tribes: The Rise and Fall of Pan-Indian Community on the Crow Reservation.* Lawrence: University Press of Kansas, 2012.

Schmidt, Alvin J. *Fraternal Organizations.* Westport, CT: Greenwood Press, 1980.

Schoenberg, Wilfred P., S. J. "Historic St. Peter's Mission: Landmark of the Jesuits and Ursulines among the Blackfeet." *Montana The Magazine of Western History*, 11, 1 (Winter, 1961): 68-85.

Siggins, Maggie. *Riel: A Life of Revolution.* Toronto: HarperCollins, 1994.

Simons, Archer O. "Report of Fort Belknap Agency." *Annual report of the commissioner of Indian affairs, for the year 1889.* Pp. 231-32.

Slotkin, Richard. *The Fatal Environment: The Myth of the Frontier in the Age of Industrialization, 1800-1890.* Norman: University of Oklahoma Press, 1998.

Smith, Diane. "Tough Trip to Publication: *Tough Trip through Paradise* and the Beautiful Wives of Andrew Garcia." *Montana The Magazine of Western History,* 58, 4 (Winter, 2008): 3-21.

Smith, Sherry L. "George Bird Grinnell and the 'Vanishing' Plains Indians." *Montana The Magazine of Western History* 50, 3 (Autumn, 2000): 18-31.

_____. "Reimagining the Indian: Charles Erskine Scott Wood and Frank Linderman." *The Pacific Northwest Quarterly* 87, 3 (Summer, 1996): 149-158.

Spence, Clark C. *Territorial Politics and Government in Montana, 1864-89.* Urbana: University of Illinois Press, 1975.

Stands in Timber, John, and Margot Liberty. *A Cheyenne Voice: The Complete John Stands in Timber Interviews.* Norman: University of Oklahoma Press, 2013.

Stegner, Wallace. *Beyond the Hundredth Meridian: John Wesley Powell and the Second Opening of the American West.* Ca. 1954. Reprint New York: Penguin, 1992.

Stuart, Granville. *Forty Years on the Frontier.* Ed. Paul C. Phillips. Cleveland: Arthur H. Clark Company, 1925.

Svingen, Orlan J. *The Northern Cheyenne Indian Reservation, 1877-1900.* Boulder: University Press of Colorado, 1993.

Swartout, Robert R., Jr. "From Guangdong to the Big Sky: The Chinese Experience in Frontier Montana." Ca. 1988. In *Montana: A Cultural Medley.* Ed. Robert R. Swartout Jr. Helena: Farcountry, 2015. Pp. 94-120.

Swibold, Dennis. L. *Copper Chorus: Mining, Politics, and the Montana Press, 1889-1959.* Helena: Montana Historical Society Press, 2006.

Taliaferro, John. *Charles M. Russell: The Life and Legend of America's Cowboy Artist.* Boston: Little, Brown, 1996.

Thompson, Sally, Kootenai Cultural Committee, and Pikunni Traditional Association. *People Before the Park: The Kootenai and Blackfeet Before Glacier Park.* Helena: Montana Historical Society Press, 2015.

Toole, K. Ross. "The Genesis of the Clark-Daly Feud." In *The Montana Past: An Anthology.* Ed. Michael Malone and Richard Roeder. Missoula: University of Montana Press, 1969. Pp. 168-180.

_____. *Montana: An Uncommon Land.* Norman: University of Oklahoma Press, 1959.

Trachtenberg, Alan. *The Incorporation of America: Culture and Society in the Gilded Age.* Ca.1982. Reprint New York: Hill and Wang, 2007.

Turner, Frederick Jackson. "The Significance of the Frontier in American History." In *The Frontier in American History.* New York: Henry Holt, 1921.

Vrooman, Nicholas C. P. *"The Whole Country was . . . 'One Robe'": The Little Shell Tribe's America.* Helena: Drumlummon Institute, 2012.

Walter, Dave. "Chief Charlo and the Salish 'Trail of Tears.'" In *More Montana Campfire Tales: Fifteen Historical Narratives.* Ed. Dave Walter. Helena: Farcountry, 2002. Pp. 53-68.

We, the Northern Cheyenne People: Our Land, Our History, Our Culture. Lame Deer: Chief Dull Knife College, 2008.

Welsh, Donald H. "Pierre Wibaux, Bad Lands Rancher." Dissertation, University of Missouri-Columbia, 1955.

White, W. Thomas. "Paris Gibson, James J. Hill & the 'New Minneapolis': The Great Falls Water Power and Townsite Company, 1882-1908." *Montana The Magazine of Western History* 33, 3 (Summer, 1983): 60-69.

Worster, Donald. *A River Running West: The Life of John Wesley Powell.* New York: Oxford University Press, 2001.

Wyman, W. P. "Report of Crow Agency." *Annual report of the commissioner of Indian affairs, for the year 1889.* Pp. 223-27.

NEWSPAPERS

Anaconda Standard
Butte Daily Miner
Butte Inter Mountain
Butte Semi-Weekly Miner
Daily Missoulian
Daily Yellowstone Journal
Fergus County Argus
Fort Benton River Press

Great Falls Leader
Great Falls Tribune
Helena Independent
Helena Weekly Herald
Livingston Daily Enterprise
Meagher County News
Missoulian
New North-west
New York Times
Philipsburg Mail
Sun River Sun

INDEX

ACKNOWLEDGMENTS

So many Montanans contributed to this project during my road trips to share *Montana 1864*, this book's predecessor and prequel, on behalf of Humanities Montana. Good folks in Bannack, Billings, Bozeman, Broadus, Butte, Cooke City, Dillon, Eureka, Fort Benton, Hamilton, Harlowton, Havre, Helena, Heron, Libby, Livingston, Lolo, Missoula, Pictograph State Park, Roscoe and White Sulphur Springs provided me essential leads and needed advice on how to make *Montana 1889* a better book. The list that follows is partial, then, but please know I'm grateful to each and every thoughtful person who shared insights into what makes readable, engaging history.

Thanks to these generous guides who took time out of busy lives to provide leads, clarify facts, answer questions, and lend moral support: Jeff Wiltse, Anya Jabour, David Moore, Mark Miller, Calvin Rice, Kim Briggeman, Karl Olson, Marsha Fulton, Sharon Ann Holt, John Clayton, Tristan Davies, Laurene DeBord, Kevin Kooistra, Cheryl Hughes, Tim McCleary, Ellen Baumler, Cathy Moser, Laurie Mercier, Bridget Kevane, Pat Munday, Megan Sanford, Tom Vitolo, Ken Robison, Jeff Birkby, Don W. De Jarnett, Roger Young, Rachel Rawn, Claudette Morton, Jackie Stoeckel, Richard Gibson, Rich Aarstad, Anthony Johnstone, Richard Littlebear, Bernard Rose, Jodie Foley, Lory Morrow, Jeff Malcomson, Ellen Crain, Roy Andes, and Aubrey Jaap.

Special thanks go to thoughtful readers who critiqued all or parts of the manuscript, saving me from false claims, misstated facts, and graceless phrasing: Kristi Hager, Chérie Newman,

Victoria Jenkins, Martin Kidston, Tim Lehman, Bruce Wendt, Robert Swartout, Nicholas Vrooman, David Mogen, Robert Brown, Jim Meinert, Jerome Greene, Donna Lucey, and Martha Kohl.

As always, my deepest gratitude goes to my family. My wife, Terry, read the manuscript carefully and listened patiently and wisely to my often rambling thoughts. Our sons, Devin and Brian, possess the intelligence, creativity, and courage to make a better future. May history truly be a guide but never a limitation.

ABOUT THE AUTHOR

Ken Egan Jr. is the author of *Montana 1864: Indians, Emigrants, and Gold in the Territorial Year*, *Hope and Dread in Montana Literature* and *The Riven Home: Narrative Rivalry in the American Renaissance,* as well as many articles on western American literature. He co-edited *Writers Under the Rims: A Yellowstone County Anthology.* After completing his Ph.D. in American literature at the University of Wisconsin-Madison, he taught college literature and writing for 25 years. He currently serves as executive director of Humanities Montana, which provides programs and grants on history, literature, Native American Studies, and more all over the state of Montana.

ALSO BY KEN EGAN JR.

A Clash of Nations

In 1864, vast herds of buffalo roamed the northern plains and numerous Native American nations lived on both sides of the Continental Divide. Lewis and Clark had come and gone, and so had most of the fur trappers and mountain men. The land that would become Montana was mostly the wild landscape it had been for millennia.

That all changed in a single year—1864—because of gold, the Civil War, and the relentless push of white Americans into Indian lands. By the end of that remarkable year, Montana was the newest United States territory.

Writer and scholar Ken Egan Jr. captures this momentous year with a tapestry of riveting stories about Indians, traders, gold miners, trail blazers, fortune-seekers, settlers, Vigilantes, and outlaws—the characters who changed Montana, and those who resisted the change with words and war.

"This is the best Montana history I've read in years. Bravo!"

—Brian Shovers, Montana Historical Society Librarian

"*Montana 1864* is as important as it is entertaining. The format, the author's voice, and his uncanny knack for making connections between characters and the world at large offer a change in pitch that just may do a great service to the historiography of the state for years to come."

—*Big Sky Journal*

RIVERBEND
PUBLISHING

WWW.RIVERBENDPUBLISHING.COM